Flexible Work Arrangements

Flexible Work Arrangements
Managing The Work–Family Boundary

BENJAMIN H. GOTTLIEB
University of Guelph, Ontario, Canada

E. KEVIN KELLOWAY
University of Guelph, Ontario, Canada

And

ELIZABETH J. BARHAM
Federal University of Sao Carlos, Brazil

JOHN WILEY & SONS
Chichester · New York · Weinheim · Brisbane · Singapore · Toronto

National   01243 779777
International (+44) 1243 779777
e-mail (for orders and customer service enquiries):
cs-books@wiley.co.uk
Visit our Home Page on http://www.wiley.co.uk
or http://www.wiley.com

Other Wiley Editorial Offices

John Wiley & Sons, Inc., 605 Third Avenue,
New York, NY 10158-0012, USA

WILEY-VCH Verlag GmbH

Pappelallee 3, D-69469 Weinheim, Germany

Jacaranda Wiley Ltd, 33 Park Road, Milton,
Queensland 4064, Australia

John Wiley & Sons (Asia) Pte Ltd, 2 Clementi Loop #02-01,
Jin Xing Distripark, Singapore 129809

John Wiley & Sons (Canada) Ltd, 22 Worcester Road,
Rexdale, Ontario M9W 1L1, Canada

Library of Congress Cataloguing-in-publication Data
Gottlieb, Benjamin H.
    Flexible work arrangements: managing the work-family boundary / Benjamin H.
Gottlieb, E. Kevin Kelloway, and Elizabeth J. Barham.
        p.   cm.—(Wiley series in work, well-being, and stress)
    Includes bibliographical references and index.
    ISBN 0-471-96228-7 (pbk.)
    1. Hours of labor, Flexible—Canada.   2. Work and family—Canada. I. Kelloway, E.
Kevin.   II. Barham, Elizabeth J.   III. Series.
HD5109.2.C2G67   1998
331.25'72'0971—dc21   97–34185
                                                                                          CIP

British Library Cataloguing in Publication Data

A catalogue record for this book is available from the British Library

ISBN 0-471-96228-7

Contents

About the Authors

Benjamin H. Gottlieb is a Professor in the Psychology Department at the University of Guelph, in Guelph, Ontario, Canada. He received his PhD from the University of Michigan, and is a Fellow in both the American and Canadian Psychological Associations. Professor Gottlieb has authored or edited four books and numerous scholarly papers on the subjects of work and family balance, social support, and coping with chronic stress. He consults with organizations and human service agencies that wish to design and implement flexible work arrangements.

E. Kevin Kelloway is a Professor in the Department of Psychology at the University of Guelph. Dr Kelloway holds a PhD in Organizational Psychology from Queen's University. He is co-author of *The Union and Its Members: A Psychological Approach* (Oxford University Press) and co-editor of the book series *Advanced Topics in Organizational Behavior* (Sage Publications). Dr Kelloway has been a consultant to both government and private industry in the areas of leadership development, attitude/morale surveys, and data analysis. He has published numerous research articles and book chapters dealing with various aspects of organizational psychology including unionization, occupational stress, and attitude–behaviour relationships in organizations.

Elizabeth J. Barham is an Assistant Professor in the Psychology Department at the Federal University of Sao Carlos, in Brazil. She received her doctoral degree from the University of Guelph, where she worked with the Canadian Aging Research Network

(CARNET) as a Doctoral Fellow. Her research continues to centre on the topics of work and family balance, eldercare, and the effects of flexible work arrangements.

Foreword

In our organization, interest in work–family practices emerged from a strong corporate core value of concern for people. It was the 1970s and 1980s, an era when there were fewer competitive pressures than is true of our current business reality. Like many other leading organizations, we introduced flexitime and other alternative work arrangements. Although never presented as support for women, flexibility had a distinct gender flavour and made us a very attractive employer. We felt we were doing the right thing, and we had the foresight and resources to do it. However, we viewed these new arrangements as privileges and as minor deviations from a world that was built around a 9 to 5, 5-day working week.

Competition has intensified in the 1990s. The increasing demands on our workforce made it very difficult for employees to maintain a healthy balance between their work and family responsibilities. We heard concerns about this from many quarters of the organization, and our indicators drove home the message even further. They suggested that workplace stress, absenteeism, and dissatisfaction were mounting. Hence, at a time when the need to improve productivity was most acute, we were faced with the increasing costs that stemmed from employee role strain. Interestingly, at that time, our external consultants advised us not to ask our workforce about the stress issuing from their efforts to harmonize work and family. They suggested we did not want the data, and even if we did, there was nothing we could do about it anyway, so why ask?

When we were presented with the opportunity to work with

CARNET: the Canadian Aging Research Network in the early 1990s, we were aware that there was a significant gap between what we said about flexibility and how our people experienced it. Through an initial company-wide survey, we obtained a comprehensive view of the personal and organizational issues surrounding our employees' 'struggle to juggle'. The survey was followed up with focus groups, some composed of managers and some composed of employees involved in eldercare, childcare or both types of caregiving. Collectively, these sources of information helped us to explore, debate, and gain a deeper understanding of the issues. We learned that we have a large 'sandwich generation' composed of people who have dual caregiving responsibilities. We learned that flexibility was not an issue of concern to women alone, but to all employees who had outside commitments and responsibilities. We also learned that, when employees had confidence in the support and understanding they would receive from the company if their family demands collided with their job performance, they experienced less stress. And in particular, our focus groups taught us to recognize the importance of the sanction and support for flexibility provided (or withheld) by senior management, and their implications for our corporate culture.

All of this information not only gave us an opportunity to revisit our practices, but also to engage the management team in a dialogue. We wanted to raise management's consciousness of the issues, while also empowering them to bend the rules in ways that offered triple-win solutions—for the manager, the employee, and the company. Although each individual must take the initiative required to establish a healthy balance between the job and the rest of life, management must provide the opportunity, understanding, and ongoing support needed to successfully implement a variety of flexible arrangements. Moreover, whether they are short-term or continuing arrangements, and whether they involve a reduction of the hours of work or more freedom in scheduling the hours, these arrangements must still be predicated on a commitment to excellence. This is what makes for an effective partnership, namely the adoption of a common set of goals and mutual responsiveness to personal and job expectations. With CARNET's help, we also found ways to challenge some lingering vestiges of old thinking on management's part; that face time is a measure of value and that long hours are a measure of loyalty and promotability.

Our collaboration with CARNET also reached beyond efforts to change attitudes and the signals sent by management. We faced practical problems such as a Human Resources Information System which was based on full-time jobs and a conventional full-time schedule. Batch runs each night limited work carried out late in the day. Even the legislative framework in which we operated as an employer was structured around this standard pattern. Hence, as we moved toward a more flexible workplace, we confronted numerous barriers that needed to be overcome. This work continues today and is made even more daunting by the heavy work demands and multiple, layered changes faced today by so many organizations. However, as this volume reveals, flexible work arrangements can take many shapes and can offer new solutions to ease the process of organizational change. The learnings, recommendations, and measurement strategies offered by the authors constitute an indispensable toolkit for companies and managers who wish to reinvent themselves along more flexible lines.

The collision of work and family demands is occurring at a time when business can afford it least. The organizational costs of imbalance are reflected in diminished performance, the loss of key talent, absenteeism, disability, and flagging morale. The pressures on business to improve productivity and competitiveness are intense and unrelenting. Employers need the best from their workforces. At the same time, the workforce has balance needs that, if unresolved, drain energy and focus from work responsibilities. This book's important message is that effective, meaningful, and strategically integrated work and family policies and practices are key elements of the solution.

Kathie Must, Human Resources Executive
Waterloo, Ontario, Canada

Preface

This volume reflects a felicitous collaboration among its three authors. Capitalizing on differences in our training backgrounds and consulting expertise, we have attempted to develop a sound and comprehensive understanding of the organizational and personal processes entailed in planning and implementing flexible work arrangements. As applied social psychologists, Drs Gottlieb and Barham have specialized knowledge of the interpersonal dimensions of the process of organizational change, particularly the attitudinal shifts and behavioural adjustments that are entailed in the introduction of new ways of structuring work schedules. As an organizational and industrial psychologist, Dr Kelloway has brought his expertise in the measurement of employee needs, managerial practices, and organizational outcomes to the challenges of empirically documenting the ways people and workplaces are transformed with enlarged flexibility. Our complementary perspectives and skills, along with the sheer pleasure of working together as a team, have made our collaboration both intellectually and personally rewarding.

Our work has been generously supported by many individuals and organizations. Funding for the several surveys, focus groups, and interviews, as well as for our administrative and research infrastructure, was provided by the Government of Canada's Networks of Centres of Excellence (NCE) programme. As members of one of these networks, namely the Canadian Aging Research Network (CARNET), we joined several eminent social scientists across Canada in an integrated research programme investigating ways of promoting independence and productivity in an aging society. Our own node in this network concentrated on strategies of harmonizing employees' job, family, and personal responsibilities. These strategies included, but were not limited to, the development of flexible work arrangements in several large, private sector organizations. We are grateful to Dr Anne Martin-Matthews, the leader of our node of CARNET, for her support of our work. We also wish to acknowledge the important contributions made to the original *Work and Family Survey* by our colleagues, Drs Monique Gignac, Alun Joseph, Carolyn Rosenthal, and Victor Ujimoto. Dr Gignac also played an important role in the planning of the *Workplace Flexibility Study*.

We are especially grateful to Kathie Must, Senior Human Resources Executive with the Mutual Group, who entered into a four-year partnership with us that extended through the full cycle of planning, implementing, and developing a corporate policy for flexible work arrangements. Ms Must gave us the benefit of her many years of strategic planning in the human resources area, and inspired us by the vision and passion with which she championed the case for flexibility in her organization. We also extend special thanks to her for graciously agreeing to write the Foreword. We are also most grateful to the Human Resources personnel at the Canadian Imperial Bank of Commerce, who sponsored and provided the technical assistance for the *Workplace Flexibility Study*, our evaluation of the impacts of flexible work arrangements.

We also express our appreciation to Dr Cary Cooper, the series editor, and Ms Claire Plimmer, the publishing editor, for their guidance and forebearance during the course of this project. Finally, we wish to thank all those employees and managers who took the time and care to attend our focus groups, complete our surveys, and share with us their frustrations and successes in implementing and optimizing flexible work arrangements.

Benjamin H. Gottlieb
E. Kevin Kelloway
Elizabeth Barham

Guelph, Ontario
May, 1997

Series Preface

There has been a growing concern about the costs of workplace stress among employers, unions and policy makers not only in North America but also throughout Europe. The changing nature of work with more downsizing, short term contracts, part time working and the huge influx of working women has meant that the public and private sector in the developed world is under increasing pressure. The purpose of this series is to explore the kinds of issues confronted daily by human resource professionals in their effort to improve well being at work. Each book highlights a particular issue and then provides some possible solutions and strategies from an HRM perspective. The books will explore such themes as employee assistance programmes and workplace counselling, managing trauma in the workplace, employee absenteeism, managing attendance, diagnosing organizational stress, assessing corporate culture, creating flexible work arrangements to combat stress and many others.

This book explores one of the most important concerns of most contemporary companies, how to help dual career couples, and the organization, create a more flexible work culture to enable employees to better balance work and family commitments. It not only raises the issues but also provides insights about 'best practice' in using flexible work arrangements to combat stress.

I hope this series will provide the reader with a grasp of the 'people issues' in today's organizations, as well as some sound suggestions and strategies about dealing with them. John Ruskin wrote about work and well being as long ago as 1851, when he said 'in order that people may be happy in their work, these three things are needed: they must be fit for it; they must not do too much of it; and they must have a sense of success in it.' For organizations to truly understand this, is the challenge for the next millennium.

Cary L. Cooper

1
Defining and Making the Case for Flexible Work Arrangements

INTRODUCTION

Susan Miller is the Manager of Health Claims at the head office of a large insurance company. She supervises 75 claim processors, and another 35 telephone clerks who respond to customer inquiries about their claims between the hours of 7:00 and 19:00. All but three of these 110 employees are women, and the vast majority of them are mothers as well. When the telephone service was first introduced, Susan had to determine how to deploy her staff to cover the 12 hour service day. She decided to present the problem to the entire department, and came away from the meeting with a list of people who wanted to work according to a variety of different schedules. Some preferred swing shifts that allowed them to go home for a few hours in the middle of the day to prepare the evening dinner, look in on a frail parent, or simply recover from the morning's telephone inquiries. Others preferred to work three 12-hour shifts, and then have a 4-day break that would give them the large block of time they needed to complete assignments for evening courses in which they had enrolled. Still others decided that this was an opportune time to request a part-time arrangement that would involve sharing a job with a co-worker who also wanted to cut back her hours at work.

The result is that there are now about thirty different *flexitime* arrangements, and sixteen part-time employees, half of whom share jobs. An added bonus is that the *job sharing* arrangement created several new vacancies in the unit, allowing Susan to absorb some employees who had lost their positions elsewhere at head office due to restructuring. Equally important, the results of the last employee morale survey showed dramatic improvements in Susan's performance ratings as well as in employee job satisfaction. There was also an upturn in customer satisfaction ratings, and gains in the unit's speed of processing claims. The popularity of this increased flexibility is reflected in Susan's annual report to her manager: 'If we ever went back to a rigid schedule, it would be a sad day. We have learned that one size doesn't fit all'.

Resilient Tire and Booms Ltd manufactures solid rubber tires for forklift trucks and other heavy equipment, as well as a variety of elevated platforms that are used by utility, construction, and stadium workers. The company has an aggressive marketing team of 38 sales representatives who work out of offices that were built onto the manufacturing plant, and who are deployed throughout North America. In addition, 175 employees work on the plant floor. Orders have been increasing rapidly over the past two years, facing management with the task of determining how to utilize more fully the manufacturing equipment without having to pay high overtime rates to employees or leaving them with less time for their families. At the same time, a small scale expansion of the manufacturing space was required to accommodate the addition of some new equipment.

Management met these challenges in two ways. First, since the sales representatives were on the road so much of the time, management decided to expand the plant by colonizing all but five of the sales force's offices. The remaining offices could be used as temporary quarters when a representative needed to come into head office. Hence, the sales division could primarily work from their homes, with the company providing equipment and furniture that they could use to furbish home offices. Each *telecommuter* received a computer with fax modem, a telephone answering machine, basic office furniture, and a modest home remodelling subsidy. Second, to make optimal use of the shop equipment, the company moved to a 24-hour a day operation, seven days a week by implementing two versions of a *compressed work week.* Two platoons of plant employees work four 11-hour shifts from Monday to Thursday, workers switching shifts every two weeks. These workers are rewarded for their intensive labour with a three-day weekend. Employees on the two weekend shifts work three 12-hour shifts, but are paid for 40 hours of work, and then get four days off.

Both of these novel arrangements have yielded benefits for the company and its employees. Since the sales staff were used to operating on a solo basis, and because they often regretted spending so much time away from home, they felt that the telecommuting arrangement gave them greater flexibility to respond to their family's needs when they were not on the road. It also improved their efficiency because they no longer had to shuttle back and forth between office and home. With free access to fax, e-mail, and courier services, they could communicate promptly and succinctly with co-workers and senior management, file their monthly reports, and still have the time to attend an after school conference with their child's teacher. From management's perspective, huge capital cost savings were realized by annexing the sales department's offices, with no adverse effects on the speed or accuracy of communication.

Similarly, the new shiftwork arrangements were greeted very favourably by management and employees alike. Less time was wasted reheating the heavy presses that vulcanize the rubber because there were no longer any shutdowns, and like the sales staff, the majority of the workers cherished the sustained time they had to attend to family responsibilities or to engage in leisure or educational activities. Commenting on the large number of employees who coveted the 36-hour weekend shift, the plant's general manager remarked: '*A lot of our people are dads and the others take up studies or work on projects around their homes or in their communities. Or a guy can really work on his golf game spending that kind of time on the course during the week.*'

AIMS AND BACKGROUND OF THE BOOK

This book is largely addressed to managers, supervisors, and human resources personnel who wish to familiarize themselves with the variety of ways in which flexible work arrangements, such as those identified in the preceding case examples, can be used as strategic tools to address productivity, morale, cost, and employee development issues. The book aims to equip these individuals with the knowledge, insights, and tools required to:

- identify employees who are experiencing stress resulting from episodic or ongoing conflicts between their jobs and their personal lives;
- negotiate and implement flexible work arrangements that optimize benefits for both the employee and the employer;
- monitor and evaluate the personal and organizational impacts of policies and practices related to flexible work arrangements; and
- develop mechanisms to ensure that the process and outcomes of flexible work arrangements are consistent with principles of equity and fairness, and that they are aligned with the organization's guiding credo.

The book is based largely on our extensive history of consultation with numerous employers in both the public and private sectors regarding techniques of assessing the need for and implementing flexible work arrangements and related work–family initiatives. Our approach is unique by virtue of its strong empirical grounding. Typically, we begin by conducting a systematic assessment of the work-life pressures that are prevalent among employees, gauging the personal and organizational costs incurred by such stress, and assessing the need for and appeal of existing and potential strategies of alleviating and preventing these pressures. Through the use of interviews and focus groups, we gather qualitative data on these subjects, while also compiling quantitative data through periodic surveys of the workforce. We confer with senior management and human resources personnel about ways of embedding work–life balance (ie, the relation of work to life) within the corporate culture, and about how to promote and reward flexibility on the part of management. Finally, we provide technical assistance for customizing resource materials and evaluative tools which will enable employers to proactively design flexible work arrangements and continuously monitor their effectiveness.

SOCIAL AND ORGANIZATIONAL TRENDS
FAVOURING FLEXIBLE WORK ARRANGEMENTS

The preceding two case examples illustrate the many creative ways in which employers are using flexible work arrangements as strategic management tools. Just as organizations devise new products and services to meet the needs of their external environments, so too are they innovating new policies and programmes to meet the shifting needs of their employees and to attract the talent that will give them a competitive edge. According to Hewitt Associates' (1995) survey of 1050 major US employers, 67% of companies offer some type of flexible work arrangement. Flexitime is the most prevalent arrangement, offered by 73% of those employers, followed by job sharing (36%), compressed work weeks (21%), and telecommuting (19%), usually involving work at home arrangements.

Particularly in an era of corporate downsizing and restructuring, job sharing arrangements represent a way of retaining valued personnel on a part-time basis rather than dismissing them, with the attendant threat and demoralization that are aroused among other employees. When companies decide to contract in size, whether on a temporary or permanent basis, the flexibility that is provided by a programme of reduced hours can lower payroll costs while retaining highly skilled employees. Similarly, at a time when companies are extending their hours of customer service, many offering 'round the clock response capability, there is a call for more flexible scheduling, including restructured full-time hours and unconventional part-time hours. For example, financial services are now widely available on a 24-hour-a-day basis, partly because of their globalization and partly because customers expect their needs to be serviced at any time of the day or night. Flexible schedules and innovative part-time arrangements permit managers to achieve broader or more intensive coverage during periods of high demand, as well as to relax their staffing during slower periods.

Flexible work arrangements have also given many employers the competitive edge in recruiting qualified personnel and in retaining employees in whom they have made a significant investment. This is because compensation and benefits are often very similar across employers, making the quality of working life and the balance between work and the rest of life more salient bases for distinguishing among employers. Especially for companies that recruit for jobs requiring the specialized skills of 'bright collar' or information age workers, or employers that draw on a labour pool composed of a high proportion of people with family responsibilities, flexible schedules offer a recruitment advantage. In addition, companies that create more part-time positions by implementing job sharing arrangements thereby establish a mechanism for cross training, since more employees can rotate through these positions. Finally, telecommuting not only offers companies cost savings by virtue of reducing the expense of office space, but also reduces parking costs and automobile pollution. In fact, in ten heavily polluted regions of the United States, the federal Clean Air Act of 1990 requires companies with at least 100 employees to design 'trip reduction programs' in order to reduce solo commuting to work. The State of California has also introduced legislation that limits the number of vehicles that employers are permitted to accommodate at the workplace.

From the employees' perspective, flexible work arrangements can make a profound difference in terms of stress and the quality of life. Witness the following plea for flexitime from a bank employee who must otherwise choose between meeting her family's needs and fulfilling her job responsibilities:

> I think it would be excellent to start work at a later time in the morning. We presently start work at 8:30, which puts a strain on my family life. My family always comes first, no matter what. I give my all at my job, but if my family needs me in any way, they are top priority. We should not be criticized for having a family with needs.

Indeed, some subgroups in the workforce are at much greater risk of serious adverse health and job consequences stemming from clashes between their employment and onerous responsibilities at home and in the community. These employees include parents of young children and adolescents, individuals who provide care to elderly or disabled family members, and employees who hold positions in voluntary organizations or who are involved in continuing educational pursuits or vocational training.

However, broad demographic trends suggest that the workforce of the twenty-first century will be increasingly characterized by an older and more diverse labour pool, composed of people who have substantial family responsibilities and for whom the quality of the work environment is as important as the compensation they receive. Among the latter qualities, flexibility in the place, hours, and scheduling of work is of paramount importance. In fact, recent studies have shown that large proportions of employees are willing to trade money and advancement at work for the increased flexibility to spend time with family members and to engage in other valued activities outside their jobs (Galinsky, Bond & Friedman, 1993). For example, in our own research, we have found that 45% of men and 50% of women would turn down a promotion if the new position would leave them with less time for their personal or family life. Similarly, 32% of men and 44% of women would trade a promotion for a more flexible work schedule. We also found that 36% of men and 27% of women would take a transfer to a new location if it promised to give them more time for themselves or their families (CARNET, 1994).

In addition, in a survey of 777 Canadian organizations, aimed to document attitudes and practices related to the subject of work and family, approximately a quarter of the responding companies reported that there is a perception that employees must choose between moving up the corporate ladder and devoting time and attention to their family lives (Watson Wyatt Memorandum, 1995). Finally, a survey of the quality of working life among a nationally representative sample of US employees, revealed that 60% of respondents stated that they considered their job's effect on their personal or family life as a 'very important' factor in their decision to accept their current employment. In comparison, only 35% rated the salary or wage they were to be paid as a 'very important' factor in their employment decision (Galinsky, Bond & Friedman, 1993).

Demographic and social trends underscore the need for employers to come to terms with the personal and family challenges faced by their workforce. As elsewhere in the industrial world, Canadian women have substantially increased their participation in the labour force in the past 30 years, rising to 58% by 1991 (Lero & Johnson, 1994). Moreover, the largest increase in the rate of labour force participation has occurred among women with pre-school-age children, the rate for women with a youngest child under three years of age nearly doubling, from 32% to 62% over the 15 year period between 1976 and 1991 (Statistics Canada, 1991). Some sense of the pressure on these women is gained from data revealing that more than two-thirds of mothers with a youngest child under the age of six worked at a paid job or business on a full-time basis. The proportion of dual wage earning couples in the Canadian population is equally impressive. More than half of all married women were in the paid labour force in 1986, with almost two thirds of them (63%) being between 45 and 54 years of age. This latter statistic suggests that large numbers of employed women find themselves at a stage in the life course when they have a high probability of assuming some responsibility for the care of elderly parents, with many adding such care to the care of children who are still at home. Hence, as Martin Matthews and Rosenthal (1993) have pointed out, the 'caregiving crunch' experienced by this sandwich generation stems from the reduction of the amount of time that women can devote to assisting family members, not from any increased demands for such care. The multiple pressures that employed women face, and the toll that these pressures take on their psyches are dramatically illustrated in the following remarks of a bank employee:

> The long days—I leave for work at 7:30 and return at 6:30—leave little time for young, growing children, time for my husband, and personal time. Added requirements to take the CIM (Canadian Investment Management) course and study outside of work hours are absolutely impossible. My weekends are spent with my children and their activities, and maintaining/running my home. Personal/social time is limited as is. If I don't take the course I will receive a low rating on my annual review; it is part of my team target to complete the course. The bank is requiring that we take this course, therefore they should allow for this time, not expect me to take it out of my family time.

The case for flexibility is given even greater urgency by evidence that there is an insufficient pool of younger, entry-level workers who can replace an aging workforce. Therefore, employers need to take measures to retain their more seasoned workers, giving them the flexibility they desperately need to meet their family responsibilities and other life commitments.

All of this means that in the vast majority of Canadian families with children, no parent stays at home. In companies with large numbers of female workers, this is evidenced by the cascade of phone calls that 'light up the switchboard' every afternoon at the time when latchkey children return home from school. It also suggests that the formerly full-time job of managing a home is now compressed into late afternoon, evening, and weekend hours, leaving less time for recovery and recuperation from job demands, much less for leisure activities with family members.

An increasing number of employers are recognizing that all employees experience periods in their life when they must grapple with emotional problems that are brought about by stressful life events and developmental turning points that affect themselves and their loved ones. Their worries about how to manage or resolve these problems cannot be confined to the hours they spend outside the workplace, and therefore they carry their personal concerns with them while at work. For example, in a study of family influences on the workplace, Crouter (1984) quotes a manufacturing plant's supervisor, who was preoccupied by concerns about his teenaged son:

> When there's strife at home, I have to consciously put it in the back of my mind. My son had a serious motorcycle accident last year, and could have died. That took its toll on my abilities to concentrate. Arguments do that, too (Crouter, 1984: 432).

In this, and many other instances of episodic or ongoing tension between work and family, organizational support and managerial flexibility can be of profound importance. This is revealed in Box 1.1, which shows that, for both employed fathers and mothers, their supervisor's understanding is among the most highly requested expression of organizational assistance (Lee, Duxbury, Higgins, & Mills, 1992). Moreover, by assisting a diverse workforce to find creative solutions to tensions between their jobs and their personal lives, employers will find themselves rewarded with a more productive, loyal and healthy pool of employees. This is vividly illustrated in the following observations of two bank employees. Whereas both employees express their appreciation of the flexibility they have been granted by the bank, the second employee also voices her concern about the absence of a career track for individuals who have job-sharing arrangements.

> Because my branch manager has given me the opportunity to work hours that suit me, I strive to do the best job that I possibly can. I would also go out of my way to do something job-related if my manager asked me to, such as extend my hours and visit customers outside the branch. Several of my 'A' clients have my home phone number, and I have no problem dealing in this way.

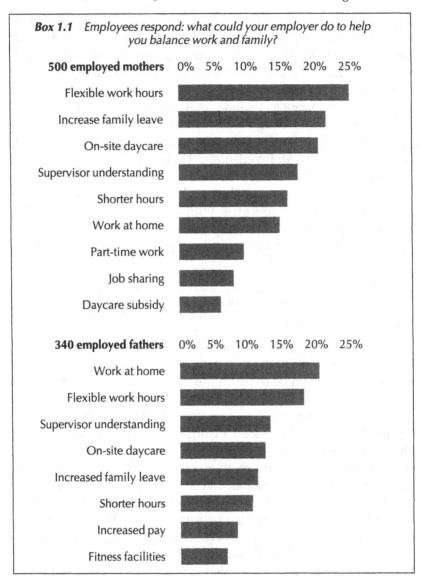

Box 1.1   Employees respond: what could your employer do to help you balance work and family?

500 employed mothers

0% 5% 10% 15% 20% 25%

- Flexible work hours
- Increase family leave
- On-site daycare
- Supervisor understanding
- Shorter hours
- Work at home
- Part-time work
- Job sharing
- Daycare subsidy

340 employed fathers

0% 5% 10% 15% 20% 25%

- Work at home
- Flexible work hours
- Supervisor understanding
- On-site daycare
- Increased family leave
- Shorter hours
- Increased pay
- Fitness facilities

The second employee also feels indebted to the bank for her arrangement, but adds a caveat:

> I feel very lucky to be employed on a job-sharing basis. It provides me the flexibility I require to balance my family life and run a smooth household. It also allows me to give 100% to the bank while I'm at work because I can

prepare so well for the days I do work. I become frustrated sometimes at lost opportunities for advancement, but understand that this is my decision right now and if I stay informed and trained, I would be able to slide in if opportunity arose and I so desired.

Since caregiving continues to be largely gender defined in western cultures, organizations that employ large numbers of women are particularly sensitive to the strains that arise when domestic and paid work collide. These organizations, including banks, insurance companies, educational institutions, retailers, and hospitals have therefore been the pioneers in establishing a range of flexible work arrangements. To the extent that these arrangements succeed in mitigating the stress arising from the cross pressures between the job and demands at home, they may prevent lost productivity due to physical or mental absenteeism, tardiness, or exhaustion, the loss of motivation and interest at work, and ultimately, the loss of jobs and the considerable financial investments entailed in training employees for those jobs.

From a more positive perspective, the introduction of flexible work arrangements, and their customization to the individual's needs and lifestyle, can signal to employees that their company is committed to helping them achieve a more harmonious and healthy balance between their personal and work lives. Moreover, to the extent that considerations of flexibility enter into managers' performance appraisals, appear in annual morale surveys, and are enshrined in human resource policies, employees will view management as more responsive and compassionate, and they will demonstrate more loyalty and commitment. Moreover, according to the National Study of the Changing Workforce, the most attractive employers are those who offer flexible work arrangements. The study's findings revealed that 60% of employees took their present job because they anticipated it would minimize any adverse effects on their personal and family lives (Galinsky, Bond & Friedman, 1993).

In what follows, we define each type of flexible work arrangement (FWA), describing variations in its structure, and briefly considering its benefits for employees and management. Box 1.2 summarizes this information. Chapter Two provides greater detail about the potential costs and benefits of these work arrangements.

Box 1.2   *Definitions of Alternative Work Arrangements*

Flexitime

start and/or end the work day earlier (or later) than usual
  Pros: allows employees to co-ordinate work hours with other
         obligations
  Cons: (a) some flexitime policies are not very flexible; the employee
         must report for work at a fixed time; (b) working time is at the
         work site

Compressed hours

work fewer (or no) hours some days, and longer hours on other days *(e.g.,
work 37.5 hrs. in 4 days, with 1 day off)*
  Pros: blocks of time off work, at times when services can be accessed
  Cons: (a) it is difficult for employees to make caregiving arrangements
         for the extra portion of their working days; (b) employees are
         often extremely fatigued at the end of long work days

Telecommuting

work from home for all or part of the work week
  Pros: (a) enables employees to assist a dependent for limited periods
         of time throughout the day; (b) commuters can reduce their
         travel
  Cons: reduces the employee's visibility and social integration at work

Part-time

work less than 30 hours a week
  Pros: enables those with time-consuming domestic or community
         responsibilities to be employed
  Cons: in some organizations, part-time positions may have reduced or
         no fringe benefits, lower pay, and/or lower job security

Job-sharing

share the responsibility and benefits of one full-time position with another
employee
  Pros: may permit higher-level employees to work part-time hours
  Cons: the job performance of each employee may not be
         distinguished; this is problematic if employees make unequal
         contributions

DEFINITIONS OF FLEXIBLE WORK ARRANGEMENTS

Flexitime

The most prevalent alternative work arrangement, flexitime or
flexible work hours, typically consists of flexible workday start
and finish times. Most organizations that offer flexitime require

all employees to be on the job during a set of core hours, but allow employees more choice over their work schedules on either side of these core hours. Flexitime does not alter the total number of hours for which the employee was hired, but most flexitime arrangements include schemes for logging surplus and deficit hours they may have incurred. For example, if, during a given week, an employee's family demands require her to arrive at work when core hours begin at 10:00 and to leave when core hours end at 16:00, then over a five-day work week, she will accrue a deficit of 10 hours in her regular 40-hour work week. She can then repay her debt by extending her hours through the two flexitime periods (08:00 to 10:00, and 16:00 to 18:00) during another week, or by working extra hours on certain days in the months ahead. Most flexitime plans give employees the option of accumulating or banking extra hours as credits to be used within a designated time period, and repaying owed hours as deficits. Rarely can employees receive overtime pay for their credited hours. In most flexitime plans, workers and managers agree in advance on a maximum number of carry-over hours from one period to the next, and a minimum notice period for time off when credits can be spent.

Flexible hours can be extended even more by further dividing core hours into two periods, one in the morning and one in the afternoon, with a flexible lunch period in between. This provides a third period of flexible hours, when employees can tend to tasks and domestic chores, look in on elderly relatives, or have lunch with a child.

Like other flexible work arrangements, the degree of variation in employees' hours of work that can be accommodated depends on the number of daily hours the organization operates, the hours each employee is required to be present, the extent to which satisfaction of other workers' and customers' needs depends on interaction with the employee, and the manager's tolerance of work schedule variability. Some managers prefer predictability and therefore ask their employees to commit to a flexitime schedule that is permanent or at least fixed for a period of time. Sometimes referred to as 'staggered hours', this fixed flexitime arrangement does not involve any carry-over of excess hours or shortfalls. Other managers are prepared to approve a truly variable flexitime arrangement whereby employees schedule their work hours on a daily basis, as their needs dictate. However, some positions preclude such variability because employees must be on the job at the same time every day. For example, a school principal is unlikely to approve a variable flexitime arrangement for a normal classroom teacher, but could consider staggered hours which ensure the teacher's presence during specified hours.

Flexitime arrangements are attractive to employers who need to maintain extended hours of operation or respond to fluctuating levels of service or product demand. As one bank manager commented when asked about how an employee was faring in her new flexitime arrangement:

> Our branch and this employee believe that customer service is our number one priority. Therefore, we do our best to accommodate our clients, including working earlier or later to meet with them at their convenience, or occasionally on Saturdays if needed. This employee is single and has somewhat more flexibility than many others, but she still highly values personal time, and we respect her professional and personal commitments (CARNET, 1995).

Flexitime arrangements are also perceived to be a means of reducing tardiness, absenteeism, and turnover, and improving employees' time management skills. Moreover, since some employees' flexitime hours occur when their manager is not present (before the manager's arrival or after the manager's departure), managers must be prepared to either relinquish or delegate supervision of the employee. By the same token, when supervisory time is reduced, it is important for flexitime users to discuss how their managers will evaluate their performance. Ideally, there should be agreement that performance will be assessed in terms of what is accomplished rather than when it is accomplished.

Flexible time arrangements not only give employees a greater sense of control over their hours of work, but also give employees formal recognition and compensation for the extra hours they devote to their jobs. For example, the following bank employee should not have to regularly donate time to her branch in order to achieve superior performance appraisals; in a flexitime arrangement, she would be credited for her extra hours. However, at present, she describes her predicament this way:

> For the last two years I have been rated '4' (high performer) on annual reviews. I am convinced that this would *not* be so if I left each day at 5:00 p.m. No matter how I attempt to manage my time daily, my manager or

other employees demand my time at 4:50 p.m., and I rarely leave before 5:45 p.m. If I were to refuse to stay to assist them or attend a meeting, my performance would be perceived as 'not committed' to the success of the branch or team.

Flexitime also enables employees to meet a variety of responsibilities at home and in the community during the standard 9:00 to 17:00 workday. Instead of having to spend most of the weekend attending to banking, shopping, and domestic chores, much of this work can be accomplished during the non-core hours of the work week. Moreover, in urban areas, flexitime can help employees avoid rush hour traffic, thereby reducing their commuting time. In addition, for a diverse workforce, flexitime offers a means of facilitating participation in religious and cultural practices. For example, Jewish employees who wish to leave work early on Friday afternoons in order to observe the sabbath can be accommodated by drawing on their credited hours. In this way, flexible hours can also help an organization achieve its employment equity goals. Similarly, flexitime can be used for employees who wish to upgrade their skills or continue their education by enrolling in a course scheduled for three hours on a weekday afternoon.

Job Sharing

Job sharing is an arrangement in which two people voluntarily share the responsibilities, salary, and (pro-rated) benefits of one full-time position, each working part-time on a conventional basis. Job sharing creates normal part-time employment opportunities where there is a need for a full-time position. It differs from other part-time work by virtue of the coordinated approach to job responsibilities that it requires.

There is great variability in the ways the time and the demands of a job are shared. Time need not be shared on a 50:50 basis, but can vary in proportions usually depending on the needs of the job sharers. For example, two employees, each of whom has a preschool child, may wish to spend more time with their children, but neither wishes to quit work or take a leave of absence. Together, they submit a proposal to their manager which specifies how they will share the time and responsibilities of a single position. Whereas some proposals may involve workers sharing the same responsibilities, others may call for them to assume complementary job functions. Partners who have the same skills and experience may fully share all activities, divide them according to each party's interests and aptitudes, or accept equal assignments of projects, with each of the sharers taking responsibility for his or her own projects and sharing responsibility for the general duties of their common position. Partners with different skills and experience can engage in complementary activities that reflect each partner's strengths, or they can fully share all activities, with each learning from the other's area of special competence, or divide the work on a senior–junior basis. It follows that job sharers may be jointly accountable for some aspects of the job and individually accountable for others.

The job sharing schedule can also be highly variable because it is usually carefully tailored to the two parties' personal circumstances and lifestyles. Those employees who opt for a weekly 50:50 time split may each work for two and a half days or divide the schedule into mornings and afternoons. However, they may also choose to work alternate weeks, or three days on and two days off followed by two days on and three off.

The quality of the working relationship between the job sharers is a critical determinant of its success. Experience reveals that the optimal process for the development of a job sharing arrangement is when the two parties jointly apply to share a job after they have confirmed their compatibility and decided how to divide their work, and coordinate with one another and with their manager and co-workers. When this is not possible, such as when an agreement to share a job has been reached between one employee and the employer before identifying a partner, or when a new partner has to be found to replace one who has left, it is best to involve the job sharers in the selection of their partners. No manager wants to assume the extra work of resolving differences between job sharers, and therefore employees who have not 'done their homework' with one another before approaching their manager are unlikely to receive a positive response.

For employers, job sharing arrangements hold the potential advantages of greater productivity due to the increased energy that part-time employees can bring to their work, greater job commitment because the sharers have a stake in making the arrangement succeed, better coverage of the job because the sharers can step in for one another when need be rather than turning to less qualified relief personnel, and improved problem-solving and innovation, because these assets are required to make the job sharing arrangement work. As one bank manager commented:

> In my opinion, the success of job sharing is through having very compatible employees who maintain open communication with each other, as well as a manager who adjusts to setting expectations for one position and coaches two people for the results (CARNET, 1995).

In addition, it is noteworthy that many managers claim that the combined hours and contributions of job sharers far exceed those resulting from one individual occupying a full-time job. In short, because job sharers tend to devote more time to the job than they are paid for, it is usually a value-added arrangement.

For employees, job sharing is a creative way of achieving a healthier balance between paid employment and the demands issuing from family and community life. It can offer considerable flexibility in scheduling time at work, and combined with the reduced hours of paid employment, it usually results in more productivity on the job, greater job satisfaction, and less stress and burnout. Job sharers also benefit from the opportunity to learn from the complementary skills and experiences of their partners, and have the advantage of exchanging mutual support and encouragement. Job sharing is a viable option for individuals who are unable to work full-time due to a disability or during a period of convalescence following hospitalization.

The problems that can arise in job sharing arrangements include difficulties in communication and collaboration between the partners, which can not only make them less productive, but also create problems for managers and co-workers. It has also been suggested that, because they are on a reduced hours schedule, job sharers are perceived to have less commitment to the job and may not be taken as seriously as full-time employees. For these reasons, job sharers sometimes find it difficult to get promoted or to advance as a team, and therefore they need to discuss with their managers how this arrangement might affect their career path. Finally, although in principle unions and other employee associations support the idea of job sharing as a way of harmonizing employment and family responsibilities, they are apprehensive about the possibility that employers will use this arrangement to convert full-time positions into part-time jobs. In addition, they want assurances that job sharing will not circumvent the terms of a collective agreement that govern hiring, seniority, promotion, and benefit levels and continuity (Labour Canada, 1990).

Telecommuting

Sometimes referred to as telework, sometimes as flexiplace, and sometimes simply as work-at-home, telecommuting is an arrangement in which an employee works at home, in a satellite office, or at a customer's location for part or all of the work week. When they are not in the central office, telecommuters communicate with their co-workers and managers by means of phone, computer modem, and fax.

Telecommuting schedules can vary widely, from every other week, to every other day, to full-time. Some employers allow employees to use telecommuting arrangements whenever they want or need to work at home, whereas others stipulate that a telecommuter must attend the workplace for a minimum number of consecutive hours each week. Full-time telecommuters and their managers usually set up a roster of face-to-face meetings at the central office in order to preserve the necessary personal dimension of office communication.

Telecommuting helps commuters to reduce their commuting time and travel costs, and it is said to relieve traffic congestion in densely populated areas, and even diminish suburban crime by keeping more people in their home neighbourhoods during the day. It also offers increased flexibility for many types of sales and service activities, such as insurance, financial, and real estate sales. In addition, it affords opportunities for better coordination of employees' work schedules with their personal and family needs. For example, the case for telecommuting on a part-time or as-needed basis is poignantly expressed in the following quotation of a female bank employee:

> I want to be able to work more hours, but because my children are so young, and young only once, I also want to be home with them on a part-time basis. If I had a computer to work on at home, there is plenty of

work I could do in the evening or on weekends (with compensation of course). As well, if one of my children were too sick to go to the caregiver or school, and I was unable to go into work, I could at least get some work done at home with a computer instead of none and be stressed out the next day because of work load.

Whereas some employees have regular weekly telecommuting schedules, others have been granted permission to work at home whenever family demands intensify, such as when a child or other family member becomes ill, as long as they alert their co-workers and managers regarding their whereabouts. Employees whose jobs involve a great deal of 'head down' work, such as planning, budgeting, computer programming, and writing, claim that they are more productive when they can work alone at home. More generally, because telework is performed independently, telecommuters must be engaged in work that involves at least some autonomous tasks.

Employees who work at home need a proper work setting for their comfort, safety, and productivity, including sufficient lighting, office furnishings and equipment. In terms of their personal qualities, telecommuters need to have strong work habits on the one hand, and the ability to discern when to stop work and turn their attention to home and family. Since there is the risk that telework will spill over and encroach on more family time than would a conventional work arrangement, the teleworker must know how to set appropriate limits on the workday. Telework is particularly well suited to employees who are self-disciplined and self-directed. Clearly, they must also be employees who have earned their manager's trust through good performance.

Some organizations have established eligibility criteria for employees applying for telework. For example, in the United States, Steelcase Inc., a designer and manufacturer of office furniture, has set the following five requirements: employees must perform an independent task as part of their larger job specifications; they must have completed a six-month probationary period with the company; they must gain the approval of their immediate supervisor; they must have a good performance record; and they must have a suitable work area at home or in another location. Based on the company's extensive experience with telecommuting, Steelcase has also generated a set of guidelines to promote the success of this arrangement (see Box 1.3).

Box 1.3   Guidelines for Telecommuters

- Adopt a 'contract mentality', in which both the telecommuter and the manager look at the work agenda as though it were a consultant's proposal.
- Establish 'checkpoints' to ensure that work progress continues to meet the needs of the company and the telecommuter.
- Communicate, in writing, each Monday morning, to outline expected results of work in the week ahead.
- Plan on regularly scheduled, face-to-face meetings with one's supervisor/manager. Support of managers and co-workers is essential, as they often act as representatives for the telecommuter in the workplace and can reflect acceptance of the work arrangement.
- Plan to attend regular team or group meetings at the company office.
- Set aside a separate room, or a part of a room, specifically for work, taking into consideration privacy, permanence, professionalism, and productivity.
- Use technology, such as electronic mail, to update managers on daily work activities that are performed.
- Invite co-workers and managers to the home office for periodic meetings.
- Share work experiences with other telecommuters and staff.
- Manage yourself by being proactive, anticipating developments, and communicating effectively and consistently with all others involved.

In a two year study of telework conducted by the Public Service Alliance of Canada, the union representing the largest number of federal employees, the following were the most frequently cited reasons for telework's appeal (Johnson, 1994):

- it eliminates long distance commuting to work;
- it prevents people from having to keep their children in day care centres for up to 10 or 11 hours a day;
- it allows parents to be home for their children after school;
- it gives employees the flexibility they want to schedule their daily work;
- it allows employees to respond more quickly to family emergencies because they are closer to their homes and communities;
- it lets people who regularly work overtime put in the extra hours at home.

At the same time, many of the preceding factors were cited as sources of difficulty with telework. For example, this arrangement does not eliminate the need for or cost of childcare services since it is rarely possible to combine paid labour and the care of young children at home. In addition, the vast majority of teleworkers in this study reported that this arrangement had been established in order to meet increased productivity expectations on the part of their employer. Many respondents stated that, in order to meet deadlines and complete tasks that they had not been able to finish during the regular workday, they regularly worked unpaid overtime hours in the evening at home. In fact, many admitted that they would work less overtime if the work were not so portable. Our own study of almost 2000 employees revealed that those who had worked at home for any period of time during the prior six months averaged a 41.3 hour work week, as compared to an average work week of 35.8 hours for those who had not (CARNET, 1993). In short, telecommuters put in almost another full day of work each week.

From a union standpoint, the risk is that telework may be a stepping stone to increased contracting out of services that are performed by non-unionized workers who are lower paid and who receive few if any benefits. Unions fear the possibility that employers will cut loose unionized workers and transform them into contractors. Therefore, through the collective bargaining process, union members want specific wage, benefit, and job protections. They also want to ensure that telework does not undermine union solidarity by isolating workers from one another. In fact, isolation from colleagues and office politics is often cited as a significant cost of telework. When employees are 'out of the loop', they miss opportunities for taking on new assignments, competing for vacant positions, networking, and following new developments. This is why companies like Steelcase advise teleworkers to spend a certain number of consecutive hours at the central office each week.

As further elaborated in Chapter Two, the telecommuting option also challenges managers to determine who is capable of working at home, how these employees' work will be monitored and evaluated, and how to develop mechanisms to facilitate regular and smooth communications with telecommuters, and between them and both internal and external customers. Clearly, telework is poorly suited to jobs that regularly call for certain kinds of teamwork activities, or that require frequent access to confidential files, documents, or data that cannot be accessed at home even by means of computer modem. In situations where telecommuters can access confidential information, they must understand and comply with information privacy and security operating procedures.

Hotelling

Hotelling is a recently coined term that refers to an arrangement that designates temporary office space for employees who normally work at home or elsewhere. Also called 'alternative officing', hotelling allows employees to call ahead to reserve a work station or office for a few hours, days or even weeks, when they need to be on site. The hotelling administrator assigns the space, puts the employee's name on the door, programs the telephone for the employee's usual (home) office number, and sees that any special equipment such as a computer is installed. Some organizations provide lockers for regular 'hotellers', where these employees store any documents they may need.

Hotelling is gaining popularity among companies with large numbers of employees whose work requires portability. For example, it has been estimated that the offices of people involved in field sales, consulting, project management, and customer service are not utilized as much as 70% of the day. As the case example of Resilient Tires and Booms illustrates, cost savings result from using space more efficiently, including a reduction in the number of permanent offices.

Compressed Work Week

This is an arrangement whereby a standard work week is compacted into fewer than five days by extending the length of the work days. The most common patterns are four ten-hour days, three twelve-hour days, and the increasingly popular 9/80 formula, which involves a week of four nine-hour days plus a fifth eight-hour day, followed by a week of four 9-hour days (with a free day in the second week). Although the four-day work week usually includes a predetermined day off, flexibility can be increased by enabling employees to choose their day off. Some employers have implemented compressed work weeks in the summer months in order to provide employees with longer weekends and to save on labour costs during slack times of the year.

From the employers' perspective, compressed work weeks allow manufacturing operations to be used for longer periods, with fewer startups and shutdowns. However, a 1989 national survey showed that the manufacturing sector was only slightly more likely to use compressed work weeks than firms in the service, financial, or insurance industries. Hewitt Associates' 1995 survey documented that 21% of the responding organizations used this work arrangement. The business case for compressed work weeks is principally based on employers' efforts to decrease the costs of overtime and to allocate labour more efficiently. For example, it can be used to optimize staffing levels during periods of peak activity. This is illustrated by an insurance company which placed its group health claims department on a compressed work week because of the large number of claims that flowed into the unit on Mondays and the small number that arrived on Fridays. Since the unit had set a goal of processing claims and issuing payment within 48 hours of receipt, the majority of the staff worked ten hour days from Monday to Thursday, leaving only a skeleton staff to process Friday's claims.

From the employee's perspective, compressed work weeks are a mixed blessing. On the one hand, they offer additional and longer periods of time away from work, with no reduction of pay. On the other hand, many employees, particularly older workers, complain about the fatigue that sets in toward the end of the longer work day, with a concomittant decline in productivity. Unions have registered their concern about the stress, fatigue, and long-term adverse health effects of compressed work weeks, as well as their encroachment on overtime. However, when compressed work schedules do not conflict with existing labour agreements, union attitudes are shaped by the perceived benefits to employees, including more family time and less commuting stress.

OVERVIEW OF THE VOLUME

Chapter Two is devoted to a more detailed discussion of the ways in which flexible work arrangements can meet personal and organizational needs, and help employees achieve a healthier balance between their jobs and their family and community responsibilities. We discuss the numerous factors that give rise to clashes between work and family life, and we discuss differences in the sources and in the organizational and personal consequences of these clashes. The chapter also spotlights the extra tensions that women experience as a function of the onerous caregiving responsibilities they tend to assume at home. It distinguishes between the demands of caring for children and the demands of 'eldercare', and calls for different organizational responses to these two caregiving contexts. We conclude with a systematic overview of the ways in which flexible work arrangements can prevent and mitigate the adverse effects of job–family conflicts while meeting the competitive needs of industry.

Chapter Three presents a step-by-step, comprehensive approach to the process of planning, negotiating, implementing, and evaluating flexible work arrangements. It is organized into two sections, the first describing a policy planning phase that includes a critical pilot test of the new policy. The second, implementation phase draws managers and employees into a collaborative and mutually responsive process that begins with a consideration of the business case for greater flexibility and ends with a contract that sets out the terms and conditions of the new work arrangement.

In the fourth chapter, we review the present state of knowledge about the effects of flexible work arrangements, and present the findings of two major surveys investigating the characteristics of employees who use different types of arrangements. Equally important, we draw on the results of a pioneering study in which we examined the impact of flexible work arrangements on such personal outcomes as stress and work–family balance, and on such organizational outcomes as absenteeism and productivity. We show that the benefits of workplace flexibility depend on the degree of choice and control that is given to employees in selecting arrangements that fit their needs and lifestyles.

Chapter Five provides a set of guidelines for management training on the subject of workplace flexibility and job–family balance. We highlight the kinds of information managers need and the types of training experiences that are most useful to them. Equally important, we discuss the need for a sea change in managers' attitudes toward unconventional patterns and schedules of work, as well as ways of overcoming their resistance to new ways of working. The chapter also includes a section containing sage advice from the users of flexible arrangements, their managers and co-workers, drawn from the many focus groups and private interviews we have held.

The sixth and final chapter offers a compendium of the measurement tools we have developed for clients who wished to plan and implement flexible work arrangements. It presents many of the questions and scales we have designed and refined to measure employees' need for such flexibility, as well as to assess the impact of new and more flexible initiatives. We are persuaded that the rigour and precision with which these tools gauge the phenomena of interest give our work its unique scholarly character and give our clients a reliable and scientific basis for formulating policy and effecting planned change.

2

How Flexible Work Arrangements Can Address Personal and Organizational Needs

Although percentages vary from one continent to the next, the majority of men and women who live in Great Britain, Europe, and North America participate in the paid labour force, occupying full-time positions. In spite of the increased size of the paid workforce brought about by the enlarged participation of women, and in spite of immense technological changes that have led to substantial increases in productivity, the number and scheduling of hours worked by full-time employees have remained essentially unchanged since the 1950s. Employers justify adherence to this work pattern partly on the basis of the need to meet mounting competitive pressures, and partly on the basis of the largely unquestioned and untested belief that maximum productivity is achieved with full-time employees who work a standard schedule.

Many employers and managers lack sufficient information about the psychological benefits and cost savings that can result from initiatives that give employees more control over how, where, and when they perform their duties. Many do not fully appreciate the wide array of organizational costs that can result from policies and practices that do not directly address the impact of personal life issues, especially family issues, on the workplace. A variety of accommodations in the structure of work are particularly needed in organizations with large proportions of either older or younger workers, since they tend to be in a life stage that involves onerous responsibilities for the care of young children or elderly family members. Likewise, employees need a better understanding of the ways in which flexible work arrangements and other workplace practices can reduce the strain they experience from tensions across the job–family boundary.

This chapter begins by examining the multi-role nature of the lives of today's employees, and the impacts of conflicts among job, family, and other personal commitments on employees. Given the rising prevalence of eldercare responsibilities, the chapter features a special section examining the differences between caring for children and elderly family members, and their implications for workplace policies and supports. Next, the nature and sources of work–family conflicts are presented, and the organizational and job opportunity costs associated with such conflicts are considered. The chapter concludes by addressing the ways in which flexible work arrangements can help reduce job–family stress, and yield strategic business advantages. The shortcomings of these arrangements are also described, along with optimal strategies of implementing them.

MULTIPLE ROLES AND RESPONSIBILITIES OF EMPLOYEES

Historically, work and family have not only been viewed as separate, complementary spheres of involvement, but also as segregated by gender (Gutek, Nakamura & Nieva, 1981). In the 1950s, men usually had only one major responsibility: their job. Moreover, what minimal domestic and family duties they did assume were quickly transferred to their wives when job responsibilities became more onerous or when the scheduling of job tasks conflicted with demands at home. In short, men assigned first priority to their role in the paid labour force, whereas women assumed responsibility for unpaid family caregiving and domestic work.

Furthermore, employers helped maintain the sharp psychological separation of these two spheres by treating family matters as categorically inappropriate intrusions in the workplace. Family caregiving and domestic work were viewed as personal and private matters. A day-to-day connection between work and family existed only insofar as it was the wife's responsibility to deal with the domestic chores and schedules needed to ensure that her husband was ready for work each day. The wife's grace and skill in hosting her husband's business associates or clients at home also was an important factor in gaining higher-level job positions. By definition, if not in actual experience, work did not conflict with family needs, but 'insufficient' support at home might impair the job prospects of an otherwise promising employee.

Much has changed since the 1950s. Today, the majority of employees occupy dual or even multiple roles; most employees must both earn a living and meet numerous family and household obligations. In addition, a significant percentage are pursuing further education or participating in activities or voluntary organizations in their communities. Employees' level of involvement in each of these roles varies over the life course, and from one individual to the next. However, for most labour force participants, their paid employment and their family involvements are the two central and most valued bases of their identities.

The transition from gender-segregated to multi-role participation in job and family duties is still in progress, however, past beliefs and practices continue to bear their mark on current role definitions and behaviours. For example, despite enormous increases in women's participation in the paid labour market, society still perceives domestic work and family care as women's primary preserves. Studies show that women continue to spend significantly more time than their husbands engaged in family-care and domestic labour (Blair & Lichter, 1991; Merderer, 1993). An American study reveals that only 10% of dual-earner couples share the housework equally, if time spent on childcare is not considered (Ferree, 1991). In addition to housework and caregiving, women in the paid labour force are also responsible for home management. This includes seeing to their children's extracurricular activities and organizing the family's social calendar. In short, family life continues to be sustained largely by women who assume the lion's share of the care of children and elderly relatives, as well as the cooking, cleaning, laundry, and sundry additional household tasks.

In addition to differences between men and women in the amount of domestic work they perform, there are differences in the kinds of tasks for which they are most likely to be responsible, and resulting differences in the time periods during which men versus women must be available to the family. Women are more likely than men to have responsibilities for fixed-time, repetitive tasks such as meal preparation, as well as for family health care, which includes caring for family members who fall ill or who are emotionally distressed. More than 25 years ago, Hall (1972) pointed out that this difference in types of responsibilities means that women are more likely than men to have to cope with family-related interruptions while in their place of employment. As discussed further in this chapter, it is the simultaneous occupancy of job and family roles rather than their sequential occupancy that drives up both the personal and organizational costs experienced by women compared with men.

Furthermore, women are far more likely than men to have a supporter role in their spousal relationship. Women typically provide greater practical and emotional assistance to their husbands than they receive in return (Thompson & Walker, 1989). Women are also more likely than men to accommodate their own vocational wants and needs to their spouse's job or career demands and aspirations.

When all the time consumed by these various domestic and family obligations is taken into account, the result is what Hochschild (1989) has called the 'second shift', referring to a pattern of full days of paid work followed by full evenings and weekends filled with unpaid family and domestic work. For those with extensive family and job demands, unscheduled discretionary time is at a minimum. Thus, any potential increases in job responsibilities require careful consideration of the trade-offs involved, since spending more time in one sphere usually means spending less time in the other.

Although employed women continue to have more onerous domestic responsibilities than men, some observers have suggested that their plight is partially offset by increases in the availability of childcare services. However, such services tend to be unevenly distributed, too costly for working class families, and of uncertain quality. Families that have more than one pre-school child generally cannot afford childcare. For example, in Canada, a country considered to have progressive social welfare policies, the National Child Care Information Centre reported that, in 1991, only 15% of the 2.2 million children 12 years of age or younger who required care were actually served by licensed care facilities (Health and Welfare Canada, 1991). In addition, the Canadian National Child Care Study found that 90% of parents were unable to find suitable childcare arrangements for their children because they could not find affordable, high-quality caregivers (Lero et al., 1992). More directly relevant to the subject of alternative work arrangements, the latter study also found that one out of six dual-earner couples with children under the age of 13 deliberately arranged their work schedules so that one parent was available for childcare when the other was working. Although such 'off-shifting' arrangements may save childcare costs, they place the parental relationship at risk by virtue of the limited time that is left for the partners to spend together. The situation is no better for parents of older children because there are few after-school programmes that provide opportunities for school-age children and youths to make constructive use of their free time. This applies with extra force to families living in low income urban and isolated rural areas (Carnegie Council on Adolescent Development, 1992).

Impacts of Gender Differences at Home on Employment Patterns

All of these differences in men's and women's home-based responsibilities show up in their employment patterns, with a far higher percentage of women seeking and holding part-time jobs and other types of non-traditional work schedules and insecure attachments to the workforce (Lero & Johnson, 1994). No wonder, then, that most of the research on the subject of work and family balance, as well as the attention it has received from employers, centres largely on married women. They are the employees who suffer the highest levels of conflict, overload, and stress, largely because of the responsibilities they assume for their families and their jobs.

ELDERCARE: NOT THE SAME AS CHILDCARE

Historically, employers have equated work–family stress with conflicts between job demands and responsibilities for the care of children. However, the growth in the size and the greater longevity of the oldest segment of the population means that an increasing number of employees will face decisions about whether and how to house and care for elderly relatives who are frail, disabled, or who suffer from chronic, debilitating ailments. Since it appears that social norms of filial obligation (caring for one's parents) are just as compelling as norms regarding childcare responsibilities, an increasing proportion of employees will find themselves confronting and managing health crises of elderly relatives. In short, now and even more so in the future, a growing number of employees will become engaged in 'eldercare'. Employees and managers alike need to know more about the demands associated with such care, and the options for meeting these demands.

What is Eldercare?

Typically, researchers define two types of eldercare: (a) 'general eldercare', which involves assistance with keeping the elderly relative's household running; and (b) 'personal eldercare', which involves both general eldercare and nursing-care assistance. 'General eldercare' includes everything from helping an elderly relative with filling out forms, arranging appointments or services provided by others, driving him or her to these appointments, doing yard work or household repairs, helping with grocery shopping and other errands, helping with laundry or meal preparation, providing financial assistance, and so forth. The second level of caregiving, 'personal eldercare' includes all of the above (i.e. general eldercare tasks) plus help with any or all of the following: dressing, eating meals, bathing, using the toilet, taking medications, and other aspects of personal hygiene.

Study results show that there is great variability in the amount of time employees spend helping their parents or other elderly relatives. Employees who provide personal eldercare, however, are generally far more taxed by these time-consuming, quasi-

---

Box 2.1   *Who is Most Likely to Engage in Eldercare?*

Although there is a strong social norm in favour of assisting our elderly relatives, particularly our parents, several factors affect the nature and degree of responsibility that an individual will assume for elderly relatives. In addition to the gender-defined nature of eldercare, the predictors of eldercare involvement include:

- Living or working near an elderly relative's place of residence, and having few siblings who also live nearby;
- Possessing less economic means of paying for help;
- Subscribing to culturally based beliefs that make eldercare normative;
- Enjoying a long-term positive relationship with the elderly relative;
- Living in rural or sparsely populated areas that have few community services.

Although these factors increase the chances of becoming an eldercare provider, there is evidence that informal, family-provided care or the orchestration of such care on behalf of elderly relatives is a highly prevalent, normative activity. For example, Dowler, Jordan-Simpson, and Adams (1992) estimated that approximately 80% of the health care received by older adults in Canada is provided by family members.

---

nursing obligations than those providing general eldercare. Estimates from a variety of studies indicate that between 10% and 20% of the North American workforce may be providing personal eldercare. In any given workplace, the character of the labour force, in terms of age distribution, gender, and ethnic background, affects the likelihood that employees will have eldercare involvements. A brief workplace survey that selectively incorporates the assessment tools appearing in Chapter Six, can provide an estimate of the extent of employees' eldercare responsibilities.

Eldercare and the Need for FWAs

In planning FWAs for employees engaged in eldercare, it is essential for managers and human resources personnel to understand the ways in which the nature, predictability, and duration of eldercare set it apart from the demands of childcare.

First, the health problems of the elderly are usually more complex than those of children, frequently requiring a longer search for the appropriate medical specialists, as well as a longer period of illness-related dependency. Health crises may be precipitated by accidents, such as hip fractures caused by falls, or by serious illness diagnoses, such as cancer or Alzheimer's disease. In most instances, the crisis eventuates in a prolonged period of convalescence or a permanent disability which must be dealt with in addition to job responsibilities. Thus, during the initial stages of eldercare, employees may need a period of enhanced flexibility in their work scehdules in order to find the appropriate medical care for their parent and to learn about the illness and their role in its management or treatment. Once caregiving routines are established, situations that require substantial time commitments on the part of employees may necessitate temporary reductions in work responsibilities.

Second, decisions concerning how to care for one's family member typically require more discussion and negotiation in the context of eldercare than in the context of childcare. Parents typically have unilateral authority to make decisions concerning their children. Adult children caring for an elderly relative, however, have shared or secondary decision-making authority. The elderly persons themselves, along with all those who are assisting them (i.e. their employed, adult-children), are usually involved in making decisions concerning medical treatment or any modifications of the older family member's home environment. Disagreements and delays in making important decisions may lead to high levels of stress for these employees, prompting them to seek practical advice and emotional support from others. Although employees with young children usually know colleagues who are in a similar situation, those engaged in eldercare do not tend to disclose their activities, largely because they are not seen as normative responsibilities. Consequently, these employees tend to feel more emotionally isolated in this caregiving role. Workplace efforts to bring these employees together in support groups or for information seminars on eldercare-related issues can help establish workplace support networks.

A third difference between eldercare and childcare is that elderly family members are more likely to suffer from chronic health disorders that call for a variety of home and personal care services. Family caregivers must therefore make their way through the maze of services with varied eligibility criteria, find those that are best suited to their relative's needs, and then actively monitor the quality and continuity of those services. This can be a protracted and exhausting process that calls for both skill and perserverance. Moreover, it is generally far more difficult to find qualified substitute caregivers for elderly persons who are homebound than it is to find them for children. In addition, costs for childcare are likely to be much lower than for eldercare because children can more easily be cared for in groups, whereas the elderly are less likely to be mobile, and may require extensive, individual, hands-on assistance.

Furthermore, in addition to the physical discomfort and functional disability of many chronic health disorders, these conditions also detract from older persons' social and emotional quality of life, creating further needs for companionship and support from their families and from substitute caregivers. On the latter score, a greater investment of time is needed to recruit, select, instruct, and maintain the morale of substitute caregivers for the elderly than for children. Late arrivals to work, early departures, and workday interruptions can all be signs of problematic caregiving arrangements, whether it is children or elderly relatives who require sustained attention. Given the difficulty of even finding substitute caregivers for the elderly, an employer-sponsored service that provides practical assistance and guidance with this task would prove to be of enormous value.

Fourth, since elderly relatives are far more likely than young children to live in a second dwelling, separately from the employee, this often means that part or all of the work of managing a second household must be undertaken when elderly relatives become ill or frail. This may include assistance with shopping, housework, transportation, banking, and home maintenance, tasks that can absorb many hours of the employee's time (CAR-NET, 1993; Lawton & Brody, 1969). Particularly when the parent lives in another community, the time required to get to and from the parent's home and to complete all the chores that await, can cut deeply into the paid work week.

Finally, whereas children's needs are predictable because they arise in relation to a more or less normative developmental trajectory, the onset and demands of eldercare are largely unpredictable. The caregiving demands associated with eldercare usually increase over time, but with little if any forewarning.

How long the eldercare involvement will endure is also largely unpredictable. This situation calls for the preparation of well-developed back-up plans between employees and their co-workers so that, if and when the caregiving situation increases in intensity, other employees can step in to maintain key work processes.

THE NATURE OF WORK–FAMILY CONFLICTS

To date, research reveals that when conflicts occur between the job and family domains, it is the family that pays the highest toll. For example, in the first of two major surveys we conducted, a sample of 5496 employees was divided into six groups based on their dependent care involvements: employees with responsibilities for (a) childcare; (b) general eldercare (as defined earlier); (c) personal eldercare (as defined earlier); (d) both childcare and general eldercare; (e) both childcare and personal eldercare; and (f) neither childcare nor eldercare. As Figure 2.1 reveals, all groups of employees, including those who had no responsibilities for the care of children or elderly relatives, felt they were making more sacrifices and concessions in their personal lives in order to handle job tasks than they made in their jobs in order to deal with their personal responsibilities (CARNET, 1993; Duxbury, Higgins & Lee, 1994; Galinsky, Bond & Friedman, 1993). Moreover, Figure 2.2 shows that employees engaged in both personal eldercare and childcare—popularly referred to as members of the 'sandwich generation'—experience the highest levels of stress.

Job–family conflicts can originate at home or at work, they can be time-based or strain-based, short- or long-term, and they can be predictable or unexpected. For example, seasoned accountants recognize that they will face an extended period of time-based conflict that originates from their heavy workloads during the weeks preceding the year-end taxation deadline. Another time-based conflict, but one that is unpredictable, short-term, and originates at home, is exemplified by a child developing an illness on a workday and needing to be cared for at home, or when an emergency home repair is needed, such as when a water pipe bursts or the heating system malfunctions in the dead of winter.

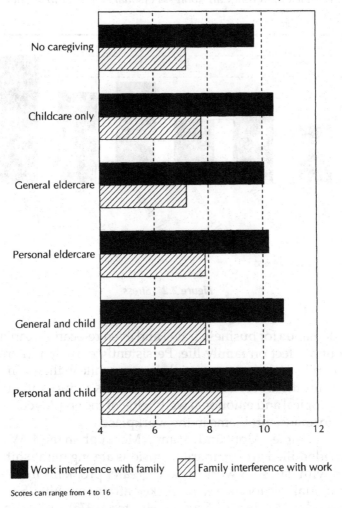

No caregiving

Childcare only

General eldercare

Personal eldercare

General and child

Personal and child

4   6   8   10   12

■ Work interference with family   ▨ Family interference with work

Scores can range from 4 to 16

Figure 2.1   *Work and family conflict*

Chronic, Time-based Conflicts

Job–family conflicts that are chronic in nature involve continuous excess demands on one's time and energy that make it impossible to fulfil either or both home and work roles effectively. Chronic, job-related conflicts arise when the timing or number of hours of absence from home interferes with family responsibilities and relationships. The number and scheduling of work hours, along

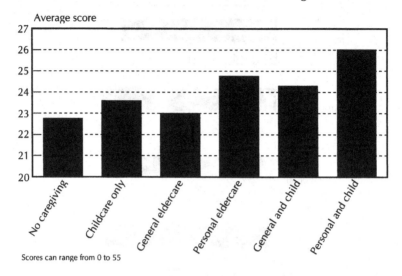

Scores can range from 0 to 55

Figure 2.2   *Stress*

with demands for business travel and even relocation, can have a profound effect on family life. Persistently curtailed interaction with family members, or mental absence while in their company, can strain these relationships. In turn, this reduces the overall psychological and emotional well-being of the employee, leading to performance problems in the workplace.

For example, Mott and Mann, McLaughlin and Warwick (1965) identified greater marital tensions among night-shift compared with day-shift workers, and greater problems in handling the parental role for men who worked afternoon shifts. Similarly, research by McCubbin, Dahl & Hunter (1975) documents the adverse effects on military families that result from the husbands'/fathers' frequent and lengthy absences due to field service.

Chronic conflicts can also derive from substantial caregiving responsibilities on the home front. For example, an injury, accident, or serious illness diagnosis of an elderly family member may initiate a lengthy period of caregiving on the part of the employee. Although the initial crisis and associated feelings of alarm may subside, the ensuing phase of sustained support can be a source of chronic stress for the employee.

This example also spotlights differences between short-term

and long-term needs for workplace flexibility. Job–home conflicts may begin as acute, short-term episodes, requiring an employee to be absent from work for a day or two, but evolve into prolonged periods of caregiving responsibility that can only be handled by reorganizing or reducing employees' job responsibilities.

Chronic, Strain-based Conflicts

In addition to, and often as a result of time-based conflicts, employees may also experience strain-based conflicts, a term referring to the spillover of thoughts and moods from one domain, job or family, into the other. For example, protracted difficulties with co-workers or with new technology at work can leave an employee tense, over-tired, irritable, and prone to over-react. This behaviour can create resentment and tension in the employee's relationships at home, and lead to poor management of family issues that need attention. By the same token, prolonged marital discord, difficulties experienced by an adolescent child, or problems arising from a family member's emotional disorder, can leave an employee with little mental energy or patience to deal with the added frustrations and demands of the job.

To some extent, family members can help one another gain relief from and find ways to manage their work-related pressures, just as co-workers may provide practical and emotional support to one another concerning problems at home. Tensions and pressures that persist, however, are the basis for chronic, stress-related conflicts. In such cases, worries arising in one domain, home or job, can be so intrusive that they interfere with the employee's ability to concentrate on, much less to enjoy, their experiences in the other domain.

All of these work–family conflicts can be distressing for employees, their families, and their work associates. Prolonged conflict and sustained efforts to manage conflict take their toll in decreased physical and mental stamina, and in conflictual relationships and impoverished role functioning at home and at work. Equally important, these conflicts can be prevented or resolved in ways that are more or less costly for employees, their families, their work associates, and their clients within and outside the workplace.

Workplace Practices Contributing to Job–Family Stress

Work–family stress often stems from workplace practices that have been carried over from the days when the division of labour on the basis of gender was the norm. Two common examples of outdated workplace expectations (in some cases, still job requirements) are that employees should make themselves available to work overtime on demand by the employer, and that employees should be available to attend meetings at virtually any hour of the workday. Today, a majority of employees face substantial difficulties and hardships when they are asked or required to arrive early or stay late on short notice.

For example, early morning and late afternoon meetings create problems when a child has to be taken to or picked up from school or daycare by particular times, or when the employee's daily routine entails an hour or more helping a parent change clothes, bathe, and prepare a meal at the beginning or end of the day. Quite apart from the sheer difficulty of finding someone else to fill in, and the impossibility of neglecting these tasks if a substitute caregiver is not available, extra meetings interrupt the employee's family-care routines. Involvement in these tasks provides the opportunity for one-to-one interaction, and may be loaded with symbolic significance concerning the employee's reliability and commitment to family members.

Extra work demands are also problematic for those who face a lengthy commute before and after work, are involved in a car pool, or rely on public transport. Since the standard formula equates career advancement with a long history of unpaid overtime, it is understandable that employees feel that their prospects for promotion will dim if they do not relegate their personal needs and family involvements to second place by putting in the extra hours. Given the tremendous stress this creates, many employees believe their employers should make a greater effort both to ensure that scheduled hours of employment are respected, and to consult employees about the timing of meetings, special assignments, and travel demands that fall outside regular work hours. As discussed in Chapter Four, management's recognition of the importance of employees' other involvements and consultation with employees, rather than the imposition of extra work, creates a climate that is hospitable to mutual flexibility.

ORGANIZATIONAL COSTS OF WORK–FAMILY STRESS

Although the majority of employees can keep up with their family's needs and adhere to fixed, full-time job schedules, a minority of employees with dependant care responsibilities will have such onerous caregiving demands that their job performance is likely to be affected. For employees who have standard, full-time schedules, the most prevalent problems arising at home include a child or parent who falls ill, substitute caregiving arrangements that break down (e.g. a paid caregiver who arrives late or calls in sick, or a daycare centre that is suddenly quarantined for two weeks due to the outbreak of an infectious disease), and a family member who has experienced a stressful life event (e.g. conflict with the law or a serious accident), or who is facing an important life transition (e.g. a parent who has been recently widowed, a parent who is moving to a residence that provides nursing care, a child who is having trouble adjusting to a new daycare centre or school, etc.). Furthermore, although the majority of employees with family dependants are able to maintain the same work patterns as those of employees without dependants, employees with family care responsibilities experience the highest levels of conflict between their jobs and family lives, and are most likely to experience a wide range of costs to their careers and personal lives.

In order to design workplace policies and supports that are realistic and useful for those with dependant care involvements, it is important to identify the types and extent of job costs they experience. Of course, employment equity considerations make it impossible to eliminate the impacts of dependant care on workplace functioning by selectively hiring and promoting employees who do not have and never will have such responsibilities. The point of reviewing the workplace impacts of dependant care, then, is to prevent or limit their adverse effects on personal and organizational functioning.

Dependant Care and Absenteeism

Returning to the findings of our Work and Family Survey, we also examined both part-day and full-day absenteeism among the members of the six groups with varied dependant care involvements (childcare, general eldercare, personal eldercare, both childcare and general eldercare, both childcare and personal eldercare, and those who had neither childcare nor eldercare responsibilities). The group that had no childcare or eldercare responsibilities provides a baseline against which to compare results for the other groups.

In terms of *part-day absenteeism*, Figure 2.3 reveals that between 38% and 52% of employees with the most demanding types of dependant care responsibilities (childcare, personal eldercare, and those with both of these responsibilities simultaneously) reported one or more interruptions of 20 minutes or longer during the previous six months, whereas a somewhat lower percentage, 21%, of the remaining respondents experienced such interruptions (those in the group with general eldercare and those without dependant care responsibilities). Generally, the same pattern applies to late arrivals at work.

In terms of *full-day absences*, Figure 2.4 shows that, compared with partial absences, percentages in all groups drop significantly. Between 11% and 18% of those with childcare or personal eldercare responsibilities reported having missed one or more full days of work during the last six months, whereas less than 5% of those in either the general eldercare group or in the group with no dependant care responsibilities reported missing one or more days of work.

Longer stretches of absenteeism, for *three or more days' absence at a time*, were not common in any group, but the group most affected was the one with personal eldercare responsibilities. Figure 2.4 shows that about 7% of this group reported longer absences, as compared with 3% or fewer of employees in all other groups reporting this type of absence.

Recognizing that employees' dependant care responsibilities change over the life course, a relatively small fraction of employees will have higher absenteeism levels due to dependant care responsibilities at any one point in time, but most employees will experience periods of elevated absenteeism during the course of their career. Thus, the key issue is how best to manage the workplace impacts of such absenteeism, not necessarily how to prevent them.

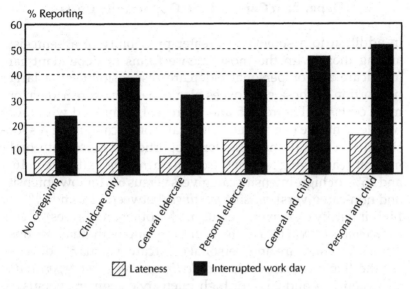

Figure 2.3   *Partial absences*

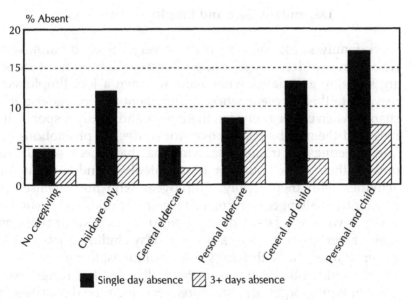

Figure 2.4   *Single and 3+ days absences*

Dependant Care and Job Opportunity Costs

In addition to a somewhat greater probability of absenteeism among those with the most intense forms of dependant care (childcare and/or personal eldercare responsibilities), a larger proportion of these employees also experience career development costs. As Figures 2.5 and 2.6 reveal, compared with those with less intense (e.g. general eldercare) or no caregiving responsibilities, a significantly greater proportion of those with high-intensity caregiving reported *declining extra projects* (between 16% and 25% for high-intensity caregivers versus 6% for low-intensity and non-caregivers), *missing meetings* (between 12% and 25% for high-intensity caregivers versus 5% for other employees), *declining business travel* (12% of those in the group with dual responsibilities for childcare and personal eldercare, versus 5% or fewer for the five other groups), and *declining promotion opportunities* (between 10% and 25% for high-intensity caregivers, versus 5% or less for low-intensity and non-caregivers).

Dependant Care and Employee Turnover

Work-family stress can also become very costly to employers who do not address these matters because high levels of stress are strongly associated with plans to leave a job. Employees reevaluate their present work arrangement and consider a job change when clashes between their work and family responsibilities lead them to be passed over for or decline promotions, to miss meetings or training sessions that have been scheduled outside their work hours, or to repeatedly abandon plans for activities with their family. Employees who find themselves constantly challenged to reconsider their priorities and to choose between work and family may be forced to postpone or abandon their career goals, to take a demotion by finding a job that is easier to integrate with family responsibilities, to suffer serious morale and family problems, or to be dismissed or resign from the employing organization. Moreover, given the disparities in men's and women's home responsibilities, it is no surprise that women are far more likely than men to experience these costs, and their implications for career advancement. The simple truth

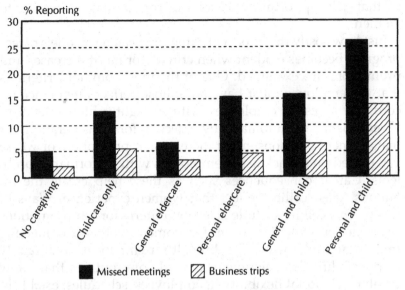

Figure 2.5   *Missed meetings and business trips*

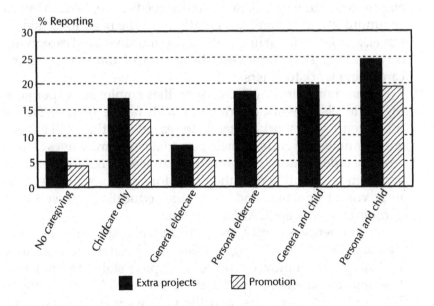

Figure 2.6   *Declined extra projects and business promotions*

is that job opportunity costs disproportionately accrue to women.

Just how costly the impact of caregiving can be on one's career progress becomes evident when criteria for merit increases and promotions are examined. One of the most common criteria is that the employee must have an almost perfect attendance record. As a result, employees with a slightly higher level of absenteeism are automatically rejected for consideration for management positions, merit increases, or promotion, or worse yet, placed on a black list of employees with performance problems. Career consequences such as these help create the infamous 'glass ceiling' effect that women experience. Ways of raising this ceiling include selection criteria for job promotions that reflect absenteeism norms for women, avoidance of meeting times that are known to be difficult for employees with family responsibilities, development of workflow routines that allow greater individual flexibility in employees' schedules, establishment of multiple workflow paths ('back-up plans') for every employee so that time-sensitive tasks can be handled by another employee when unpredictable family needs arise, investment in communications technologies that reduce the need for business travel, and investment in on-site or community-based caregiving services that give employees the option of transferring some caregiving work to others.

Furthermore, since we have seen that employees experience higher levels of work interference with family than of family interference with work, it stands to reason that they will experience a number of costs in their personal and family lives. These costs include reduced time for socializing with family members and friends, curtailment of their time for vacations, fitness activities, volunteer work, and continuing education, as well as a chronic lack of sleep (CARNET, 1993).

The frequency, severity, and outcomes of employees' job–family conflicts will be strongly influenced by numerous factors, including the employee's personal coping skills, the practical help and emotional support that are provided by family members and work associates, and the policies, services, and work arrangements that are created to accommodate the employee's lifestyle. On the latter score, the institutional resources that employers can make available to prevent or reduce work–family conflicts, and to assist employees in achieving a healthy balance between the two spheres include:

- Alternative work arrangements, such as flexitime, flexiplace, and job sharing;
- Leave arrangements for a variety of personal and family responsibilities that give employees the right to take either a few unscheduled days off, or a longer period of leave, resuming work at the same levels of pay and seniority;
- A set of 'family-friendly' benefits, such as subsidized daycare, cost-sharing for eldercare expenses, emergency childcare and eldercare services, and information or referral services regarding family-related issues.

ARRANGEMENTS THAT REDUCE WORK–FAMILY CONFLICT AND BENEFIT ORGANIZATIONS

The most important feature of flexible work arrangements of every type is that they allow employees to meet various responsibilities and priorities in their lives in ways that conventional full-time work arrangements do not permit. Flexible work arrangements are about building more degrees of freedom into the paid work component of our lives.

However, the advantages of workplace flexibility go beyond human resource issues. As previewed in Chapter One, to remain competitive, organizations must also find a means of extending their hours of service, acting quickly to keep up with changing market demands, and deploying employees in accordance with peaks and troughs in the workload. Flexible work arrangements can meet these organizational needs.

As Box 2.2 reveals, by far the most common reason why employees use flexible work arrangements is to handle family demands. A whopping 81% of employees who were using flexible work arrangements did so, at least in part, for family reasons (CARNET, 1995). However, a variety of other reasons may also prompt employees' requests for workplace flexibility. They include the desire to pursue further education, and to spend less than full-time hours on paid work activities.

Box 2.2   *What prompts employees to pursue FWAs?*

Percentage of FWA users who rate the following reasons as extremely important

Family reasons	81%
Personal reasons	39%
Non-work activities	31%
Work flow	18%
Client service	13%
Educational reasons	8%
Manager's suggestion	5%

Source: Work and Eldercare Research Group of CARNET: The Canadian Aging Research Network, 1995.

Employees who are interested in gaining further education or training presumably have greater needs for challenge, personal development, and occupational advancement. If denied the flexibility to accommodate these needs, their job satisfaction and motivation will suffer, and they will be barred from learning new information or skills that may well be of value to the organization in the future. Even if the employee is pursuing studies in a field that differs from his/her present employment, it still makes good business sense to support employee involvement in further education. A job that provides a means to another end is more motivating than a job that prevents the attainment of a desired goal. Whether for educational, personal, or family reasons, the majority of employees simply want more flexibility in their schedules so they can reduce the stress created by competing job and personal commitments.

To permit the introduction of workplace flexibility, in all its forms, a major issue that must be addressed concerns the way work is organized. Work systems based on an assembly-line pattern will require a substantial amount of re-engineering to make employee flexibility an option. When it is difficult to organize certain tasks into larger units under the responsibility of one employee, strategies that can add flexibility to a relatively rigid work system include: cross-training employees, developing a pool of supply workers, stockpiling semi-processed products at critical juncture points, and the ability to adjust the rate of production based on staffing. In addition, in many instances, flexible work arrangements require employees to carry on with work tasks at times when their manager and other co-workers are not present.

Flexitime: Letting Employees Schedule their Work

Flexitime is, by far, the work arrangement in greatest demand. It is an arrangement for employees who work full-time hours but with more control over how they schedule their time. Flexitime lets employees decide how to set up their regular work pattern so they can most efficiently organize their time, and also leaves employees with the option to respond to important demands issuing from their personal lives.

Flexitime helps reduce work–family conflicts because it enlarges employees' discretion over the scheduling of their work tasks. Within certain limits, employees can choose to work at times that best fit their before and after work involvements, and also have the opportunity to schedule tasks unrelated to their jobs during standard business hours. Avoiding rush-hour traffic to get to and from work, and avoiding queues when running errands, can yield significant time savings. In addition, employees can gain access to community services that do not operate outside of standard workday hours. For example, those with eldercare responsibilities may need to take their parent to a daytime appointment with a medical specialist who is located in another city. Being able to use their time efficiently and access the services they need helps employees manage their job better and family responsibilities and reduces their stress levels.

Of critical importance is the fact that it is not only individual employees who benefit as a result of flexitime policies, but their employing organizations as well. Organizational advantages include both improvements in human resource management and an increase in the organization's ability to respond to the demands of the marketplace.

Tardiness and absenteeism are reduced because employees can either accrue extra hours of work to prepare for an anticipated absence, or they can make up for a worktime deficit created by prior absences. Research also shows that organizations with liberal flexitime policies (i.e. policies that allow employees to set their own regular hours but also to deviate from them as needed), gain an array of psychological benefits that improve the recruitment and retention of employees. Compared with employees who must adhere to rigid start and finish times, employees who have the most discretion in their work schedules show higher levels of morale, greater job commitment, greater job satisfaction, and lower levels of stress (CARNET, 1993). Finally, productivity may also improve when employees have a block of time in the early morning or later evening when there are few interruptions, so they can deal with responsibilities that require sustained concentration.

Extended hours of operation can also bring significant business advantages. Many businesses have had to shift or extend their hours of operation to cover early morning, evening, and weekend periods, as many of today's customers are looking for 'round the clock access to goods and services. Furthermore, some organizations have employees in their head office who work in support of employees in other time zones. Other organizations offer telephone services to customers who live in a variety of time zones. Both these factors create a business need for employees who are able to work non-traditional hours.

Flexitime: Best Practices

The vast majority of flexitime users establish their own daily or weekly routine, and consistently adhere to this idiosyncratic schedule because it meshes well with their routines and responsibilities outside work. In establishing their personal schedules, they also take into regard deadlines, co-workers' schedules, and other workplace contingencies. In short, the vast majority of employees tend to go out of their way to design schedules which ensure that their absence would have the least adverse impact either on workflow or on others with whom they need to interact. As employees and managers often comment, '*If you treat people like adults, they act like adults*'.

Employers need to know this, because policies that call for managers to impose schedules on employees, and to enforce these schedules for an indefinite period of time not only leave employees with virtually no flexibility, but also deny them the choice and sense of control that have been found to be so beneficial in reducing stress. In fact, as we show in Chapter Four, even when employees have flexible work arrangements, if they have not chosen these arrangements themselves because they were hired or transferred into the arrangement by management, they do not experience the psychological benefits enjoyed by those who chose the arrangement they desired. Equally important, we found that, even if they never opt for a flexible work arrangement, employees who know that they can do so if they wish experience lower levels of stress than those whose employer has not made such an opportunity available (CARNET, 1993).

Hence, in preparation for the introduction or revamping of flexitime policies, employers and individual managers must give careful consideration to the degree of flexibility they are willing to offer employees. Assumptions about why flexible work arrangements cannot be introduced, or why they can only be introduced in a limited way need to be thoughtfully examined, inviting employees at all levels to offer suggestions about how to overcome the obstacles. The line should be drawn in a way that enhances employees' sense of control over their schedules.

Telecommuting: The Importance of Location

The telecommuting option, sometimes referred to as flexiplace, makes it possible for employees to work away from the main office at certain times, and represents another way of both reducing work–family conflicts and improving the organization's business edge. As described in Chapter One, this option helps employees reduce their travel time and associated expenses (including extended hours of childcare to cover the commuting time period). It also allows parents to plan and participate in their children's after-school activities. A work-at-home arrangement is also an attractive option for employees who need to look after a family member who is ill for an extended period of time, and who needs someone nearby for assurance and periodic assistance but only a limited amount of hands-on care during the day.

From an organizational perspective, telecommuting arrangements are advantageous when employees can work more productively at home than in the office, or when the employee would otherwise miss work time. For example, greater productivity can sometimes be achieved at home than in the regular workplace when the employee is working on a project that requires their sustained attention, particularly when there are pressing deadlines to meet. When flexiplace is not just a temporary arrangement, but a regular feature of the employee's work routine (e.g. to reduce the number of days when a long trip to the office must be made), less office and parking space in expensive commercial zones may be needed. This may or may not represent significant savings for the organization, however, since there are often other expenses associated with telecommuting, such as supporting modem links for home or satellite office computers.

Telecommuting: Best Practices

The key to the successful use of telecommuting is for both parties to think of the alternate worksite in much the same way as the regular worksite. The employer needs to take responsibility for ensuring the employee has the information, equipment, and skills that are needed to perform job tasks. The employee needs to ensure that non-job-related interruptions are minimal, that co-workers who need to receive or provide information can do so, and that the amount of time spent working is adequately monitored so that it is neither greater nor less than the time that would be worked at the primary worksite.

Part-Time Arrangements: Choosing a Balance Point

In addition to their desire for more control over their job schedules, many employees would also like more say about the amount of time they spend on paid work versus other commitments and activities. Part-time arrangements involve a reduction in the employee's hours of work, ranging from modest reductions (e.g. 90% of full-time, or seasonal arrangements such as four-day weeks during school holidays) to substantial work hour reductions (e.g. one or two days of work per week).

The primary benefit of part-time arrangements is that they can reduce the time pressures and fatigue that full-time employees often experience. These arrangements are particularly helpful for employees with time-consuming responsibilities for family caregiving and either a preference for direct involvement in caregiving or a lack of access to good-quality substitute care (e.g. due to cost or sheer lack of availability).

Part-time arrangements also have important human resource and business advantages for employers. When employees have the opportunity to retain the same job position but with a reduced workload, the costs of training a new employee can be saved. To the extent that clients (either internal or external) value interacting with this employee, retention of the employee also helps maintain the continuity of business relationships.

In addition, part-time arrangements can sometimes be implemented in ways that increase the employee's availability during peak work periods during the day or week. In some cases, part-time workers can also provide back-up support for another employee who is absent due to illness or vacation. Such staffing benefits illustrate the use of flexible work arrangements as strategic management tools, improving productivity and service levels, and reducing the costs associated with the training of less experienced temporary workers.

Finally, when part-time hours are worked on the basis of a job-share arrangement, the organization often benefits from the greater range of skills that two employees can offer rather than one, and from the help and support that these employees provide to one another when problems arise.

Part-time Employment: Best Practices

One of the greatest drawbacks of part-time arrangements is that jobs in this category are usually not integrated with the system of full-time career positions. Part-time positions are typically far less attractive than full-time positions in terms of the type of work the employee is assigned, the opportunity for advancement, and the job security and other benefits the employee is granted.

Pro-rated employee benefit packages that offer all employees certain benefits (e.g. vacation allowance) as a function of accumulated hours of work help reduce the disparities between the treatment of full- and part-time workers. Part-time workers have the same benefits as full-time workers, but earn them over a longer period of time. Cost-sharing between the employer and the worker for participation in health, life, and dental insurance plans can also provide a means of pro-rating costs for benefits that cannot be subdivided.

In addition, training programmes need to be re-designed so that part-time employees can be included. This is crucial in enabling part-time employees to keep their skills up to date and to complete training units that are pre-requisites for career advancement.

The most important factor, however, is to adopt a job sharing attitude to the formation of part-time positions. That is, the possibility of working part-time hours should exist for employees at all levels of the occupational hierarchy. Research has demonstrated that part-time workers do not lack job commitment compared with full-time workers, but simply work fewer hours. Employees in executive positions who work part-time through job sharing arrangements have demonstrated that the ability to handle multi-faceted, high-level job positions is far less a function of the hours worked than it is a function of job skills. The capabilities of the manager, systematic briefing of the job-share partner(s) at trade-over times, and effective planning of work assignments for subordinates are the factors that distinguish effective management in a job-share arrangement.

Indeed, studies of self-managing work teams have shown that increases in subordinates' latitude to independently decide how to schedule their work activities, in their self-sufficiency in resolving uncertainties about how to proceed, and in their participation in setting productivity goals and standards (work quotas and project deadlines), all tend to increase employees' sense of autonomy and control over their work. This, in turn, can increase employees' intrinsic job motivation (providing they are willing and able to learn to handle the extra responsibility), and job satisfaction.

LEAVES OF ABSENCE: EMOTIONAL TIES AND PERSONAL GOALS

A third type of flexibility of interest to employees is the possibility of setting aside work responsibilities altogether, on a temporary basis, through leaves of absence. Labour laws guaranteeing leaves of absence when a new child is born to or adopted by an employee are in force throughout North America, the United Kingdom, and Europe. The provisions of these laws vary greatly, both in terms of the duration of absence from the workplace, and the amount of compensation the employee is entitled to. All countries, however, provide the employee with a period of job-secured leave to adapt to this major life change.

Many employees with other family responsibilities, and who are affluent enough to afford it, would also like to avail themselves of a job-protected period of leave. Although the majority of employees with onerous caregiving responsibilities can manage them by using flexitime or part-time arrangements, a temporary leave of absence may be called for in caregiving situations that have strong emotional impacts or that are likely to incur substantial financial costs if someone were to be hired to provide the necessary care. For example, leaves are often requested to care for a spouse who is recuperating from a serious illness, medical operation, or accident, or for an immediate family member who is terminally ill, especially if the relative lives too far away to permit frequent visits.

In the United States, the Family and Medical Leave Act came into effect in 1993, entitling individuals in companies with 50 or more employees to a maximum of 12 weeks of unpaid leave a year for family medical emergencies. Although initially, there was considerable uncertainty about the circumstances that qualified employees for such leaves, and accompanying employer apprehension that the legislation would invite employee fraud, the record has shown that employers and employees have complied smoothly with both the spirit and the terms of the new law. It also shows that, contrary to employer expectations, the incidence of such requests is quite low. For example, a recent survey of 299 employers in the state of California revealed that two-thirds of companies have less than 1% of employees on such unpaid family leave, 16.4% have 1–2% of employees on leave, and only 1.5% of companies have more than 3% on leave (the remainder of companies could not provide such statistics) (Noble, 1994).

The business advantages of permitting employees to take such leaves are primarily related to the retention of employees who the organization would otherwise risk losing. In addition, such leaves can give lower-ranking employees an opportunity to work in jobs with higher levels of responsibility. The training and experience gained by more junior employees during these periods can improve the regular employee's access to back-up assistance when he or she returns, and also provides a chance for both the junior employee and the company to evaluate readiness for career advancement.

In early 1997, President Clinton made a further request to the US Congress to give employees 24 hours of annual unpaid leave to fulfill such family obligations as attending parent–teacher interviews, taking a child or elderly relative to the doctor or dentist, or securing a new childcare arrangement. To demonstrate his commitment to this initiative, the President sent a memorandum to the chiefs of more than 100 federal departments and agencies, requesting that they give their employees immediate access to such time off for family obligations.

Leaves of Absence: Best Practices

Leaves related to unpredictable events such as the serious illness of an immediate family member are becoming available through insurance policies. These policies provide an income to individuals who wish to take an unpaid leave in such circumstances. The payments can also be used to help cover the costs of hiring paid caregivers, medical expenses, and the like.

The logistics of introducing policies for planned leaves related to study or travel are also being considered by some organizations. Universities have long had such a professional development policy in place in the form of sabbatical leaves (usually taken in every seventh year of service). These leaves relieve professors and lecturers of their teaching and administrative responsibilities in order for them to further develop their research programmes, technical skills, or teaching practices. Proposals for policies in the private sector are exploring the possibility of allowing employees who wish to take a leave to draw four-fifths of their regular salary and deposit the remaining amount in a tax-sheltered investment account over a period of four years, making it possible for them to take a year off in the fifth year as well as reducing their taxable income each year. Variations exist in terms of the percentage of income that could be set aside and the time period for the leave. Such leaves represent a welcome, new development in organizational support for the co-existence of employees' professional and personal involvements.

SUMMARY

Leaves of absence, flexitime, telecommuting, and part-time arrangements constitute a set of alternatives to full-time work schedules that are imposed by employers. Each offers a variety of benefits in terms of reducing work–family stress and affording strategic business advantages. Although costs are involved in introducing such policies, organizations must weigh them against the costs of not making any such changes. On the human resources side, the high and still rising percentage of employees with multiple role involvements means that traditional work schedules will result in increasing costs in terms of absenteeism, turnover, and lost job opportunities. On the business operations side, the need to offer extended hours of service, to make more strategic use of employees in order to maximize efficiency, and to reduce business costs are today's organizational imperatives. Flexible work arrangements can help employers deal with both of these realities.

3
The Cycle of Planning, Implementing, and Evaluating Flexible Work Arrangements

This chapter sets out a planned and comprehensive approach to implementing and managing flexible work arrangements (FWAs). The approach is designed to ensure that the potential impacts of these arrangements on workplace routines, managers, co-workers, and employees' personal lives are carefully considered and appropriately monitored.

There are two phases in the process of introducing flexible work arrangements. The first, *policy planning phase*, involves preparing the way for the introduction of an FWA policy for the organization as a whole. This phase can be broken down into three stages, for which guidelines are provided:

- Conducting a pilot study to determine the range of FWAs that are feasible, culminating in the preparation of FWA policy recommendations;
- Soliciting feedback on, or pilot testing these policy recommendations; and
- Revising and finalizing the FWA policy guidelines and preparing for their introduction.

The second section of the chapter describes the *implementation phase* of the FWA programme, aimed to help managers and their employees successfully use these arrangements. Guidelines are also provided for the four stages of this phase:

- Clarifying managers' information needs and expectations concerning the ways FWAs will be handled in their work unit;
- Identifying ways in which managers and their employees can collaboratively design individual FWAs;
- Determining strategies of monitoring the impacts of the new arrangements; and
- Deciding how to make adjustments following an evaluation of these impacts in order to fine-tune the arrangements.

The chapter concludes with a discussion of the type of workplace climate that is hospitable to the introduction of flexible work arrangements.

PHASE ONE: PLANNING POLICY FOR THE INTRODUCTION OF FWAS

To maximize the effectiveness of flexible work arrangements, they must be carefully tailored to the job and personal life responsibilities of the user, as well as to broader aspects of the employing organization's functioning and culture, including both explicit workplace practices and implicit expectations or norms. From both management and employee perspectives, a wide range of factors affect the feasibility of FWAs. These factors include: job performance requirements, internal and external deadlines, formal workplace policies, contractual agreements with customers or external suppliers, labour law stipulations, competitor practices, and a host of individually-held beliefs about the effectiveness of various workplace routines. Thus, to introduce flexible work arrangements, or to revamp a system that excludes current FWA users from career development and management opportunities, it is necessary to attend to both individual job requirements and aspects of organizational functioning.

Planning for the introduction of an FWA policy involves three steps. First, a careful review of current workplace routines and systems must be undertaken to prepare a preliminary set of recommendations describing the types and degrees of job schedule flexibility that can be offered to employees in different job positions. Second, feedback on and testing of these recommendations is needed. Third, based on the feedback and pilot testing results, the policy guidelines will need to be revised and finalized, and prepared for dissemination throughout the organization.

Pilot Study: How Ready is the Organization for FWAs?

A systematic analysis of the degree to which work schedule alterations can be accommodated will help clarify the ground rules associated with a new level of flexibility in working hours. The more carefully and thoroughly the possibilities and limits of flexibility are considered prior to the introduction of new policy guidelines, the greater the likelihood that the policy will be well founded, well understood, and well received.

In larger workplaces, a task force should be formed to conduct the feasibility study, and back-up support arranged to cover some of the regular job responsibilities of the task force members so that they have time to conduct the review. Whether or not a systematic assessment of the sort described here is conducted, those involved in the feasibility study need to determine the kinds of alternative work arrangements that can be introduced, and the stipulations attached to each of them.

Can FWAs be Introduced?

To determine if and how FWAs can be introduced, it is necessary to gather information about each job position in the organization with respect to the following issues:

Need for Supervision or Support

Assess the extent to which the employee's ability to work productively depends on the sustained guidance, input, or resources of others. All jobs require some level of interdependence, but the need for *continuous interaction*, as compared to *episodic interaction* may call for re-engineering efforts in the operational system. In some cases, a high level of ongoing interaction is necessary only during the initial training period of a new hire. Make sure to distinguish between short-term training needs and long-term job demands.

Availability to Others

Determine the amount of time and any specific periods of the day when the employee must work with other employees, with customers, or with external organizations. Can more careful planning for the upcoming week or month reduce the amount of time when two particular employees need to be present simultaneously? What is the period of time in which the employee must accomplish his or her work so that other workers do not experience delays?

Communications

Ask about the frequency and timing of meetings that involve this employee, and the latitude that exists in setting these meeting times. Note whether these exchanges of information can be accomplished only through face-to-face interaction, or if other means of communication, such as electronic mail conferences, are also possible. Does the employee have access to these other communication systems or devices, and the knowledge to use them?

Administrative Work

Ask the employee to consider the extent to which he or she is consulted or must consult others to accomplish administrative tasks, and the deadlines that must be met for the accomplishment of this work.

Staffing Levels

Identify the peaks and troughs (during the day, week, month or year) in the work demands for this job position, so that opportunities for flexibility can be maximized at least during periods of low demand.

Cross-training

Inquire about the current availability of employees in other job positions who could substitute for this employee for brief periods (a few hours) or on a short-term basis (a few days), or who could be trained by this employee to do so.

Support Services

Consider if and how the introduction of flexible work arrangements would affect the support services provided by custodial workers, security personnel, switchboard operators, food service providers, and any transportation service operators.

Contractual Agreements

Labour laws, collective bargaining agreements, and client contracts should be reviewed to determine whether or not any of the flexible work arrangements (especially the compressed work week and part-time arrangements) will produce inequities in the treatment of employees or in responsiveness to clients. The procedures and time-frame involved in remedying inequitable stipulations in these contracts should also be specified.

When soliciting information about the previous topics from individual employees (perhaps by means of an interview or survey), ask them also to identify any problems that the introduction of FWAs might create, and their suggestions for possible solutions to these problems. This information will help the task-force prepare for the second phase of the feasibility study, namely making FWA policy recommendations.

In larger workplaces, the task force conducting the feasibility study should include representatives from each sector of the organization who will solicit and analyze information from employees in each job position, and be able to formulate policy recommendations that also take wider department functioning into account. Select task force members who have credibility with their peers, with whom employees can speak candidly, and who can hold their own with the senior managers who will review the task force's findings and recommendations.

Issues to Address in FWA Policy Recommendations

On the basis of their findings, the task force members must make recommendations about the kinds of FWAs that can be offered, and how to implement them. Specifically, they need to identify the following.

Preconditions

Any re-engineering of the work flow that is needed or equipment that must be purchased before FWAs can be introduced.

Types of Arrangements

Identify the FWAs that can be offered from among flexitime, compressed work weeks, job sharing, part-time work, telecommuting or work-at-home, and any other variations.

Limitations

Identify any job positions that will not be eligible for FWAs or circumstances that preclude their use. Indicate whether employees will be able to set up individual FWAs, or whether entire work units will have to adopt the same schedule (e.g. shift work situations). Define the earliest time an employee may begin the workday, the latest time for ending the workday, and whether or not there will be any 'core hours' (each day or week), during which all employees in either a work unit or the workplace more generally must be present (e.g. to deal with peak work periods or to reserve a period for scheduling meetings).

Terms and Conditions

Specify how 'overtime' hours will be defined under each arrangement. Is there a minimum number of hours an employee can work per day or per week? Is there a maximum number? (Note that although labour laws often stipulate that overtime wages must be paid when an employee exceeds a certain number of hours per day or per week, those organizations that offer compressed work weeks have gained special permission to re-set or waive the daily limit for employees who use this arrangement.) When introducing flexitime systems that give employees the responsibility of keeping a running record of their hours, specify how the accumulation of extra or deficit hours will be handled. If an employee accumulates extra hours, for how long can this time be carried over to use as time off, or at what point will the employer pay the employee for this overtime? What notice period is required (if any) before an employee can take time off to compensate for accumulated overtime? Will there be any restrictions on how much time can be taken off in a single block, and whether this time may be added onto a block of vacation time (a considerable advantage for those who plan to make long trips)? Similarly, if an employee has worked fewer than the number of hours for which she or he is paid, how large a deficit can be accumulated, and how much time does the employee have to reduce or eliminate the deficit before pay is deducted?

Monitoring Procedures

Does the employer plan to monitor such organizational impacts as productivity levels, lateness, sick days, or turnover? If so, are baseline data (prior to the introduction of FWAs) on these measures already available? Think carefully about how to measure certain impacts. For example, if flexitime is being introduced, how will 'lateness' be defined, given that employees will be deciding when to arrive and leave? In this case, absenteeism may need to be calculated on the basis of any deficits in hours worked per week.

Will employees be required to formally report the number of hours they have worked to management, or will an honour system be used, trusting employees to keep track of their hours? Insofar as FWAs already increase the extent to which employees assume responsibility for their own schedules, having employees monitor their own hours is in keeping with this emphasis on trust and self-management. Keep the focus on the employee's productivity, not clock watching.

Procedures for Proposing an FWA

Lay out the procedures that employees should follow in making requests for FWAs (e.g. completing a proposal that details: the change being requested, how work tasks could be re-organized to accommodate these changes, the arrangements that would need to be made with co-workers to make it feasible, and any training needs that would need to be addressed for the employee and co-workers to handle new tasks or new equipment). Apart from the employee and his or her immediate manager, it is essential to identify any other parties who must provide approval before the FWA can be initiated.

Other Resources

If the manager and employee need any further information, who can they turn to? If any disputes should arise, are there procedures in place to resolve them (e.g. ombudsperson)?

Pilot Testing the Policy Guidelines

Once the preliminary policy guidelines have been formulated, it is critical to get feedback from others. Holding formal or informal meetings (or focus groups) to discuss the guidelines with employees is probably the least time-consuming and least costly means of gaining feedback. Benchmarking, by comparing one's guidelines with those of similar workplaces, especially organizations that have comparable workflow patterns, is also instructive. The best reality check of all, however, is to give the guidelines a trial run. Whether a whole department participates in the trial, or only one employee, this is an opportunity to test and modify the new policy guidelines.

A pilot test is the most effective method of evaluating a set of preliminary guidelines for FWAs. This involves the administration of measures prior to and at the end of the test period, either by interviewing or surveying some or all of those who participated in and were affected by the new arrangements (see Chapter 6). Decide on the set of questions before starting the pilot test, so that exactly the same measures can be readministered at the end of the trial run. This will enable you to make direct, before-and-after comparisons of your job performance and morale measures. When the second wave of information is gathered, however, encourage employees to add any comments they may have about the arrangements' impacts and ways of fine-tuning their implementation, over and above the questions that are repeated from the wave one interview or survey.

Number of Employees to Evaluate

If only a few employees are trying out the arrangements, ask all of them to participate in the interviews, or to respond to the survey you prepare. If a large group of employees is participating, randomly sample employees from this group (e.g. a group of 30 would be sufficient). Note that, for a variety of reasons, some of the employees who participate in the first (pre-test) wave of interviews or surveys may not be available to participate in the second (post-test) wave. Ideally, fifteen to twenty employees will participate in both waves of the study. Thus, by including extra employees in the first wave of the study, you can increase the likelihood that you will have enough employees participating in the second wave to form credible conclusions.

A 'One-Shot' Evaluation

A somewhat less costly option is to conduct an evaluation at the conclusion of the pilot test only. In this case, you would ask employees to rate the extent to which they observed an increase, decrease, or no change in their own and others' performance on a series of measures. The problem with this 'one-shot' evaluation is that recall of past behaviour and organizational functioning is subject to distortions of various sorts, and therefore is not as accurate or detailed as reports about the current state of affairs. In addition, any differences between current and past functioning may be unintentionally exaggerated (positively or negatively) or minimized, depending on the respondent's personal stance toward the new arrangements.

Costs

Both types of evaluation, two-wave and one-shot, will require a certain investment of time to prepare an interview protocol or paper-and-pen survey, to conduct the interviews (or distribute the surveys) at one or two time points, and to analyze the results. There will also be minor costs for paper and printing, and for employee time. Allowing employees to be interviewed or to complete surveys during paid work time will vastly increase response rates. It also signals to employees that their organization is sufficiently concerned about the effective implementation of FWAs to obtain feedback on company time.

The care and effort required to prepare an interview protocol or survey for the pilot test is well spent, however, since it can also be adapted for use as an assessment tool once the official FWA programme is introduced. Indeed, it is important to conduct a systematic pilot evaluation of such an important change in the way work is organized, prior to its full introduction. Otherwise, features of the programme that could have far-reaching impacts on the organization and on employees could be overlooked.

Confidentiality

Employees will need assurances that their responses to questions will be confidential (i.e. no one other than the interviewer will know the identity of the employee who gave the interview, and only codes, not names, will be written on surveys). If you are conducting before and after interviews or surveys, each

---

Box 3.1   *Evaluating FWAs: Three Types of Questions*

Counting

Whether you are assessing the results of a pilot test of FWAs or of a full-blown, organization-wide programme, try to ensure that you use a response scale that suits the question being asked. Some survey or interview questions can be answered with a number, even if an estimate is made. Examples of questions that call for quantified responses include the number of hours employees worked during the past week, the number of 'units of work' they produced (if there is a component of their work that can be counted), the number of days they were absent from work in the previous month, and the number of occasions when their non-work commitments resulted in their missing twenty minutes or more of a work day (e.g. late arrival, early departure or an interruption during the day). Note that, for many of these questions, you will need to define a time period (e.g. during the last week, last month) for which the count should be made that is of sufficient duration for the event to have occurred but not so long (e.g. last year) that the number of occurrences can no longer be recalled with any accuracy.

Rating Scales

In addition to questions inquiring about how often certain events have happened, include questions that delve into the impacts of FWAs on the quality of the performance of certain tasks and on employees' work attitudes and well-being. To simplify and quantify the analysis of these responses, use 'fixed-format' response scales such as those that appear in the final chapter of this volume.

For questions about *quality of performance* issues (such as accuracy of work, quality of work, concentration on the job, and energy level at work), use rating scales such as the following:

1	**2**	**3**	**4**	**5**
Very low				**Very high**

For questions about employees' *morale and personal well-being* (such as the amount of job stress employees experience, the amount of fatigue they experience at work, the amount of time they are preoccupied with thoughts about their homelife responsibilities while at work, their satisfaction with their jobs, perceived support from their co-workers and manager, extent of job security, and opportunity for advancement or promotion to other job positions), use the following type of rating scale:

1	**2**	**3**	**4**	**5**
Very little				**A great deal**

(continued)

Finally, because some events are not systematically monitored, certain types of events preclude reliable reporting by employees (examples include the number of times employees were unable to attend meetings scheduled outside regular hours, declined extra assignments, missed job-related training sessions, postponed, cancelled, or declined business trips due to family demands). Responses to these questions can be handled by adopting a set of more subjective categories, such as the following:

---

1 – Never able
2 – Seldom able
3 – Sometimes able
4 – Usually able
5 – Always able

Describing

You may also want to ask a few questions that call for open-ended responses, allowing employees to describe or evaluate specific aspects of their job situation in a short, narrative style. For example, you could ask employees to describe any problems their current work schedule causes in the domain of co-worker or customer relations or in their personal life. *Free-format* responses are open-ended in nature, and are generally used to capture more qualitative, descriptive information.

It should be noted that analysis of the information obtained from these free-format questions is much more time consuming and labour intensive than analysis of the fixed format data. It is necessary to code, organize, and then interpret the themes emerging from the accounts that were generated. On the other hand, these narratives add richness and credibility to the evaluation, and can be liberally sprinkled throughout the final report as a way of bringing the quantitative data to life.

A second issue that warrants attention is that open-ended responses are also 'riskier' for employees because of the possibility that their accounts will inadvertently reveal their identity, thereby breaching their anonymity. Particularly when respondents have complaints or criticisms to offer, they are unlikely to be frank if they suspect any possibility of their identities being disclosed. Hence, when respondents are being quoted in a report, it is essential to edit out any segments of the response that could identify either the employee or others with whom the employee works.

In sum, a well crafted and efficient survey that inquires into the impact of flexible work arrangements should contain a majority of fixed response and a small number of free-response format questions. The numerical data can be quickly tabulated, summarized, and interpreted in terms of explicit response options, while greatly increasing the ease of comparing responses from different individuals and organizational units. The descriptive information provides rich contextual detail that can vastly improve the understanding and interpretation of the numerical data, and the stories authored by the respondents bring credibility and a human face to the evaluation.

(continued)

Double-barrelled questions

When preparing a set of questions, be sure to ask only one question at a time. When you ask *double barrelled* questions, such as 'On a scale of one to five, how much practical help and emotional support do you receive from your co-workers?', it is impossible to know if the employee is rating: (a) the quantity of practical help; (b) the quantity of emotional support; or (c) some idiosyncratically weighted combination of the two. Likewise, if the employee is asked to 'Rate the quality of your relationships with your *manager* and *co-workers*', it is impossible to know if the employee's answer reflects the employee's relationship with co-workers, the manager, or some complex mental calculus that takes both categories of relationship into account. Double-barrelled questions often occur when the survey designers wish to identify the causes of a particular problem. Here, the error derives from creating an item that presumes a problem exists and inquires about its cause. For example, an item asking employees to 'Rate the extent to which your family life interferes with work because your children are often ill' will elicit an uninterpretable response because employees may have focussed either on the assumption that family life interferes with work or on the reason for it. A better way to handle this type of question is to divide it into two parts, the second part contingent on replies to the first part. That is, one begins by asking whether or not or how often the employee experiences family interference with work, and then, only respondents who do experience any or a certain degree of such interference are directed to respond to the second question inquiring about the frequency with which children's illnesses cause this interference. Naturally, employees without children would be directed either to skip this question or to mark the 'not applicable' response category. Other potential causes of family interference with work can also be separately itemized and rated.

employee should be assigned a code number that can be used to match their wave one responses to their wave two responses in order to identify the changes attributable to the introduction of the FWA programme.

Different Viewpoints

Depending on the available resources, it would be useful to supplement the employees' data about their work performance with parallel information gained from their manager and selected co-workers. This requires the recruitment of someone who has the skills to analyze multi-source information. Note that questions dealing with the employees' feelings (e.g. sense of satisfaction), or ability to deal with personal life responsibilites can only be asked of the employees themselves because others cannot evaluate impacts in these domains.

Domains of Impact to Monitor

Here are some of the areas you may wish to assess when monitoring the impacts of your FWA pilot test. Each issue is raised in the form of a question to ask in a before-and-after evaluation. In a one-shot study, these questions would need to be rephrased, asking about the *impact* that the introduction of the FWA programme has had on the employee's performance in each area, either in terms of objective changes that can be quantified (e.g. 'How many departmental meetings have you had to cancel or miss in the past month compared with the number you missed in the month before you switched to flexitime?'), or in terms of subjective ratings of the direction (positive or negative) and weight of the impact. Here is an example of the latter approach: 'How has the introduction of your flexitime arrangement affected your attendance at departmental meetings?'

	−3	−2	−1	0	1	2	3	
Very negative effect				No effect			Very positive effect	

In a before-and-after study, however, questions for each wave of the study should ask about *current* performance, or events that have occurred during a period of time, such as a week or a month, immediately preceeding the evaluation. Responses at each time period can then be compared to determine various impacts, if any, resulting from the introduction of the FWA programme. When the employee's manager or co-workers are in a position to assess certain aspects of the target employee's job performance, they can complete second and third parallel versions of the employee survey. Of course, the identity of the employee who they are assessing should be plainly displayed on the survey forms, and that employee should be informed that his or her co-workers' and manager's views are being solicited.

Here are examples of different versions of questions that can be asked of employees, co-workers, and managers about different impact domains:

Work Responsibilities

Employee survey: *'Please indicate your job title, the key tasks you are responsible for, and how much of your work time you spend on each of these tasks.'*

When you are ready to analyze the study results, the answers to these three questions should be examined first. If job responsibilities have completely changed, it will not be possible to assess a variety of impacts that rely on comparing job performance levels at time one and time two, assuming that only the job schedule has changed. For example, the impact of the FWA on employee productivity or employee relations with co-workers cannot be assessed if the employee has changed to a new job in a new department.

Accomplishment of Work

Employee survey: *'Please indicate how often your work meets or exceeds job performance expectations for:'*
Manager or co-worker survey: *'Please indicate how often this employee's work meets or exceeds job performance expectations for:'*

1 = Never
2 = Seldom
3 = Sometimes
4 = Usually
5 = Always

(a) *Quality of work?*
(b) *Accuracy of work?*
(c) *Concentration on work?*
(d) *Completion of work on time?*
(e) *Keeping abreast of changes and new information?*
(f) *Quality of service provided to customers (if applicable)?*
(g) *Other? (specify)* —————————————

Employee survey: '*During the past month, how many times:*'
(a)   Were you unable to attend a work meeting that was scheduled outside your usual hours of work?
(b)   Were you unable to work extra hours (overtime) when requested to do so?
(c)   Were you unable to take on extra projects or responsibilities at work?
(d)   Were you unable to attend a training session?
(e)   Did you use a vacation day to care for a family member?
(f)   Did you lose pay because of arriving late or leaving early?
(g)   Was your work interrupted for at least 20 minutes because of responsibilities outside work?
(h)   Did you experience difficulties with your supervisor or manager because of your responsibilities outside work?

Manager survey: '*Please rate the effect this employee's work schedule has on:*'

	−3	−2	−1	0	1	2	3	
Very negative effect				No effect				Very positive effect

(a)   *The planning you do?*
(b)   *The work flow/efficiency of your unit?*
(c)   *The planning and scheduling of meetings?*
(d)   *Your ability to meet unit performance goals?*
(e)   *The morale of co-workers?*
(f)   *The amount of responsibility you can give this employee?*

   Managers are often concerned about the extra workload that FWAs may create for them. Indeed, initial re-organization will take some extra time until new routines are established, so interpret the results for this question with caution if the pilot-test period is brief.

Internal Communications

Employee survey: '*Please rate the quality of the following aspects of your relations with people at work:*'
Manager survey: '*Please rate the quality of the following aspects of this employee's relations with people at work:*'

1 = Poor
2 = Worse than average
3 = Average
4 = Better than average
5 = Excellent

(a) *Amount of communication with co-workers?*
(b) *Quality of communication with co-workers?*
(c) *Relationships with co-workers?*
(d) *Amount of communication with manager?*
(e) *Quality of communication with manager?*
(f) *Relationship with manager?*
(g) *Other? (specify)* —————————————

Customer Satisfaction

Employee survey: '*Please rate your customers' (whether internal, external, or both) satisfaction with the service you provide:*'
Manager and co-worker surveys: '*Please rate the satisfaction of this employee's customers (whether internal, external, or both) with the service he or she provides:*'

1	2	3	4	5
Very dissatisfied				Very satisfied

If contact with customers is an important aspect of an employee's work, consider distributing a brief customer satisfaction questionnaire to a small, randomly selected sample of the employee's regular customers before and after the pilot test. In this case, it would not be necessary to survey the same customers at time one as are surveyed at time two.

Employee Job Satisfaction

Employee survey: '*Please rate your satisfaction with the following aspects of your current work arrangement:*'

	1	2	3	4	5	
	Very dissatisfied				Very satisfied	

(a)   *Your job responsibilities?*
(b)   *Your income/benefits?*
(c)   *Your opportunities for career advancement?*
(d)   *Your job security?*
(e)   *The number of hours you work?*
(f)   *The scheduling of your work hours?*
(g)   *The amount of time you spend commuting?*
(h)   *Your job as a whole?*
(i)   *Your energy level?*
(j)   *Your physical health?*
(k)   *The balance you have between your job and personal life?*
(l)   *The amount of stress you feel at work?*
(m)   *The amount of stress you feel at home?*
(n)   *Other? (specify)* ————————————————

As Chapter Four reveals, evaluation studies using questions such as these to gauge the outcomes of FWAs, and drawing on the views of both users and their managers, testify to the numerous benefits that accrue from customizing job locations and schedules to individual needs and lifestyles (CARNET, 1995). Immediate gains come in the form of a variety of psychological benefits that FWA users experience, including greater enjoyment of their work, more supportive relationships with co-workers and managers, better personal health, greater sense of control over their work, and a healthier balance between their job and other personal responsibilities and commitments (CARNET, 1995). The greatest gains, however, are longer-term in nature. Employees who find it inordinately stressful to manage their lives when they have a fixed, full-time work schedule, and whose upward career mobility is restricted by 'performance problems' (e.g. tardiness, absenteeism) are able to use work arrangements that better suit the demands on their time and also lead to greater opportunities to participate in special work assignments or projects, to receive recognition for this work, and to make career advancements. These improvements lead to higher levels of organizational commitment and greater satisfaction with family life.

Duration of the Pilot Test

The duration of the pilot test largely depends on the number of employees who participate and the complexity of the change-over. Allow time to work out initial problems that arise with the change-over and to establish new routines. Customary meeting times may need to be changed, and the number of meetings may need to be reduced by making more use of alternative communication tools that can be accessed 'round the clock from both central and remote locations. Periods when coverage levels are too high or too low will also need to be adjusted, and job sharers will have to find ways of contacting one another during their off-work hours in order to deal with urgent or particularly troublesome matters. As many employees and managers who have dealt with FWAs have observed, the more employees or co-workers treat each other as responsible adults, the more responsibly they behave. Some oversights will no doubt occur, however, so ask everyone participating in the trial run to record any accommodations they have made. These observations or records can then be used to adjust the FWA policy guidelines.

Has the Programme Been Faithfully Implemented?

Another issue to investigate is whether or not the guidelines have been implemented in a manner that is faithful to their aims and procedures. To evaluate this, include some questions about it in your post-test. For example, ask employees if the policy guidelines had to be modified in any way, if they believed the guidelines were applied fairly, and if they felt they received the active cooperation and support of their manager. Employees could also be asked to comment on whether they felt that everyone affected by the FWA, including themselves, had the skills and resources (information or technical) to adapt to the new arrangements, and if not, what additional training sessions or resources are needed.

Revising and Finalizing the FWA Policy Guidelines

Use other people's feedback on the FWA policy guidelines and any pilot study results to revise the initial set of FWA policy guidelines. If feedback on certain issues is mixed, try to identify why such differing views exist. For example, if managers respond in one way and employees in another, does this point to the need for more careful articulation of the responsibilities of each party, or perhaps for training sessions that review different ways of dealing with problems that can arise? Alternatively, mixed opinions may relate to differences in the work that each group of employees is responsible for. Do employees who have been deemed ineligible for FWAs on the basis of their job position feel that there are ways of introducing a greater measure of flexibility, short of the full array of options available to those who are eligible for these arrangements? Does the new programme increase some employees' job responsibilities to the level of higher-paid employees, but without an accompanying pay increment?

Financial Resources

Some consideration also needs to be given to the financial resources that will be required to implement the FWA programme in general, and to permit the use of particular FWAs. Arrangements will need to be made for:

Policy announcement. How will the new policy guidelines be announced and disseminated, and what costs will this involve?

Support services. How will information and guidance be provided to managers and employees planning for and learning how to use FWAs (e.g. brochures and information packages, services provided by the human resource department)? For example, the Royal Bank of Canada has prepared a series of four booklets which define each type of FWA, explain how they affect employees' benefits and compensation, offer guidelines for employees and managers who wish to implement the arrangements, and even include items allowing prospective users to assess their own suitability for each FWA. Another consideration with cost implications is whether managers should be offered training sessions to help them learn about the issues they will need to deal with in negotiating new work schedules with their employees.

Employee training. How will employee training be provided for those using FWAs? Self-guiding manuals or computer programs may help with some training tasks, making it possible for employees to progress at their own pace and in accordance with their own work hours.

Technical supports. Can voice or phone-message services be offered to employees so others can relay their requests even if the employee is unavailable? Do employees have an electronic-mail system for contacting co-workers or for broadcasting important messages? Can employees access one another's work schedules (including times already booked for meetings or other tasks) on the computer, so they can identify mutually convenient meeting times? Is a pool of portable computers (and modems) available to be signed out by employees who have to stay home for a day or two, but anticipate having the time to get some work done to access information from head office, and maintain communications with co-workers? Can cost-sharing arrangements be made for employees who wish to buy a home computer or FAX machine so they can work from home on a more regular basis? How will costs associated with modem links be handled? If a formal system of time recording is envisioned, what will the costs of this system be?

Having thought about the information resources and technical supports that are needed, the task force must now issue its final recommendations and decisions. The policy guidelines should include:

Links to company ethos. There should be a positioning of the FWA programme that fits in with key company values and objectives. For example, one Canadian bank issued the following statement regarding its commitment to flexible work arrangements: 'The bank is committed to flex arrangements because they make good business sense. The corporate policy on Balancing Multiple Commitments outlines the direct relationship between helping employees balance their commitments to work, family, education and community and improved employee morale, increased productivity, and superior customer service.'

Eligibility criteria. Although you may need to adopt certain eligibility criteria, try to take a receptive approach to requests for job flexibility; show a willingness to listen to new suggestions about how to make an FWA fit a position that is currently considered ineligible. One HR specialist told company managers that they were expected to take a 'can-do' stance toward requests for FWAs, meaning that their default position should be to try to grant every request unless there are some daunting obstacles.

- Will employees in every department be eligible to use FWAs?
- Can managers use them?
- Can auxiliary staff (such as caretakers) use them?
- Can new-hires use them? (Bear in mind that the exclusion of new employees may mean losing candidates who would otherwise have been interested in the position.)
- Does the individual manager retain the right to refuse FWAs for his or her employees, or for an invididual employee?

If employees in some job positions are regarded as ineligible for some or all FWAs, invite these employees to train and apply for other job positions that do permit the use of FWAs.

Limitations. Identify any impediments that limit the amount of flexibility employees can have, such as building hours, security service hours, telephone operator hours, and computer services hours.

Accountability. In workplaces where performance reviews of managers include input from employees, consider including items that ask employees about the degree of support their manager shows toward employees who use work scheduling flexibility, and their manager's ability to adapt to schedule changes and reorganize employee responsibilities in an equitable manner. Initially, employee feedback could be used to identify managers who are most successful in handling FWAs, and who may be able to coach or mentor other managers. Later on, employee ratings could be incorporated in the performance review, making managers accountable for the development of knowledge and skills in this area (see the items assessing managerial support in Chapter Six).

PHASE TWO: IMPLEMENTING FWAS

The process of implementing FWAs involves four key steps: (a) communicating managers' *expectations* for the use and support of FWAs within the work unit; (b) collaborative *negotiation* of individual FWA arrangements to customize their structure and terms; (c) *monitoring* the impacts of the arrangement on job performance; and (d) *evaluation* of the FWA to decide whether to prolong the present arrangement, make changes to the arrangement, or terminate it.

Communicating Expectations

When the new policy guidelines are announced, it is advisable for departmental supervisors or managers to hold meetings with their own employees. In the interest of smoothly introducing FWAs into the department, these meetings should cover the following agenda items:

Internal Communications

Ask everyone to pay special attention to ensure that vital information about internal operations continues to reach all employees. This can be accomplished with a low-tech solution, such as a buddy or partner system for those who cannot be present for important meetings, and who will be updated by someone who can attend the meeting. Otherwise, there is a variety of other solutions, such as posting minutes from meetings on a bulletin board or on a computer mail system, or including such information in memos or news bulletins.

Feedback and Adjustments

Acknowledge that, like any change in procedures, most arrangements will need some tinkering before they run smoothly. Encourage employees to inform one another of any problems that schedule changes may create, and to find their own ways of avoiding or resolving these problems. Difficulties that cannot be resolved should be brought to the attention of the manager.

Extra Work

Many workplaces have long-standing overtime routines to deal with extra work. However, the introduction of FWAs may require changing these routines. Be sure that employees who continue with their regular work schedules are not expected to assume any additional responsibilities without compensation or other rewards. **The new FWA programme will be placed at risk if co-workers feel that they must pay for the flexibility granted to others.**

Proposal Format

Finally, mention any procedures employees will need to follow and forms they should complete to request an FWA. For example, one employer has prepared a worksheet for employees to complete prior to meeting with their manager to discuss arrangements for their flexible work option. It includes questions about how the new work schedule will be implemented, how the employee's normal job responsibilities will be met under the new arrangement, how communications with customers, management and co-workers will be handled, who else should be consulted about the decision, and what business advantages the new arrangement is likely to have. Once the worksheet is completed, the manager and the employee can discuss the various issues arising from the employee's responses to the questions, as well as any implications for compensation and benefits. Boxes 3.2 and 3.3 contain samples of such proposals.

Collaboratively Designing FWAs: Topics to Discuss

Managers and employees who have already implemented FWAs recommend discussing the following topics when negotiating the terms and conditions of a new FWA:

Box 3.2 *Sample proposal for flexitime*

TO: Manager, Loan Services
         Ottawa

FROM: Wordprocessor, Loan Department
         Ottawa

RE: BALANCING MULTIPLE COMMITMENTS

With reference to the above noted circular, I put forward the following proposal for your consideration and response:

Proposed Hours of Work:

Monday to Friday 7:30 to 4:00 minus one hour for lunch (including two fifteen minute breaks) equalling 7.5 working hours.

Rationale and Benefits

1. In my current poition, I have limited customer contact on a daily basis.
2. I do not depend on the Genie Bag for majority of my daily work.
3. I would be working the same number of hours each day, with the same lunch period and breaks.
4. There would be no lost time to the Bank.
5. I would be working the whole time the Bank is open with the exception of Fridays. I would be leaving one hour before the Bank closes. I do not foresee a problem with this as my customer contact is somewhat limited.
6. I believe that these hours would result in a more productive day as from 4:00 p.m. to 5:00 p.m. the volume of activity is not heavy.

In response to your memo, and subsequent discussions, I am pleased to advise your request has been approved subject to the following amendments:

Hours of Work: Monday to Friday 8:00 a.m. to 4:00 p.m.—1/2 hour for lunch.

Rationale Behind Decision: As no one is available to open the Branch prior to 8:00 a.m., an earlier start would not be appropriate. By only taking a half hour for lunch we can still meet your objective of leaving the branch by 4:00.

The above noted arrangements will be revisited in 3 months' time to ensure that the needs of all parties involved are being satisfied.

Approved by:

K. Moore

Manager Loan Services

Box 3.3 *Sample proposal for telecommuting*

TO: Community Banking Manager
FROM: Commercial Account Manager
         Montreal

In view of the new policy regarding flexible work arrangements (HR 1002-02) I wish to propose to the Bank the following:

Proposition

I would work 4 days at the office and one day at home. During the 4 days at work I would concentrate on customer service and portfolio growth whereas during the one day at home I would concentrate on administrative reports and annual reviews. I've assessed customer patterns over the last few months and it is clear that Monday through Thursday are the days that I have the greatest number of customer appointments. I have therefore chosen Friday as the flexplace day. Ms. Lavalle, with whom I have discussed my proposal, would be available on the Friday of each week to answer customer enquiries and to address urgent matters. I would be available over the phone for assistance/discussion. In the event that Ms. Lavalle was on holiday, I would work the 5th day at the office.

My Customers:

Naturally, I would not be here when clients would call on Friday. However, Ms. Lavalle would be here to help them and/or I would be in on the following Monday ready and able to be more proactive vs reactive as I would have one day per week to complete reports, annual reviews and study prospects so that I can organize the following week's customer calls. As mentioned, in the event that Ms. Lavalle was on vacation I would work from the office.

Emergencies:

I would be available at home to answer any questions. If I'm temporarily unavailable, my answering machine is in place and I will return the call as quickly as possible. Also, in the event that I am needed at the office on Friday (for courses, clients etc.) I will be available.

I consider that this arrangement will help me to better serve my customers as I will be better able to address their problems if I know that my administrative duties are up-to-date. I believe I will be able to put into place a more comprehensive business development plan for increasing my customer base. In addition, I have discussed the insurance implications of working flexiplace with my agent.

I hope that this is acceptable and I remain open to other alternatives which allow me to meet my objectives and those of our customers.

(continued)

TO: Commercial Account Manager
FROM: Community Banking Manager

RE: FLEXIBLE WORK ARRANGEMENT

We acknowledge receipt of your memo and are pleased to advise that we are in agreement to try the proposed schedule of work for four months. At that time a review will be done by all parties involved, including feedback from Ms. Lavalle. As stressed in your recommendations, customer service is and will remain our top priority and we have to be governed accordingly.

   We are confident that the proposed schedule will also permit you to meet all negotiated growth targets together with a maximum of 15% of late reviews on your portfolio's total number of accounts. Please also note that this working arrangement must not create additional administration costs i.e. long distance calls, off-site terminals etc.

   If at the end of the trial period we agree to continue the arrangement it is also agreed that one month's notice will be given if either of us feel at some point in the future that it no longer is suitable or appropriate.

New Schedule

What are the new hours the employee proposes to work? For telecommuting arrangements, how much of the employee's work time will be spent at the regular worksite and how much will be spent working from home? Will this vary from week to week?

   Will the employee need to make any special arrangements with co-workers, such as designating someone who will pass on information from meetings, take messages from others when the employee is off-site, and handle certain issues during periods of the business day when the employee is absent?

Job Responsibilities

Will the employee continue to carry the same job responsibilites, or will some tasks need to be transferred to or traded with those of other employees? For part-time arrangements, if the employee wishes to reduce his or her hours of work, what responsibilities will be retained, and who would be qualified to handle the remaining work?

Financial Implications

Do any of the proposed changes in the nature of the employee's responsibilites have implications for the employee's or a co-worker's pay level?

For those employees requesting part-time and compressed work week arrangements, it is important to discuss the employee's availability to work overtime, and how overtime pay will be calculated How will the new arrangement affect vacation time, and disability and sick leaves?

Communications

What changes will be needed to ensure optimal communication between the employee and his or her: (a) co-workers; (b) 'customers' (internal or external); and (c) manager? Discuss any new routines the employee should adopt to keep in touch with each of these parties, and any changes that could be made to regular meeting times to accommodate this and other employees' schedules. The employee should inform customers or co-workers of work schedule changes, so they can make their own adjustments. The employee should let their co-workers and customers know who to contact at times when he or she will be absent.

Productivity Checks

To address any concerns about immediate adverse impacts on productivity, discuss ways of monitoring the employee's progress once he or she starts to use the FWA. To do this properly, you will need measures of the employee's productivity *before* the arrangement starts that can also be taken once the employee switches over to the FWA. This will help avoid problems with inaccurate recall of productivity levels prior to the change. Be sure to discuss any plans to use these measures during a 'trial period', at the end of which a final decision would be made as to whether to give full approval to, modify, or terminate the employee's FWA. Take into account other organizational changes that may adversely affect the employee's job performance during the trial period, since they must be distinguished from the effects of the FWA. If other changes are occurring, compare the employee's performance with the performance of one of his or her co-workers who has similar job responsibilities, but who has maintained a standard work schedule.

Consequences of Unsuccessful FWAs

Generally, an employee using an arrangement that creates problems which cannot be resolved is required to return to his or her original work schedule. If this is impossible (e.g. a decision to work part-time following the birth of a child), then the manager must weigh the costs of terminating the employee against the costs associated with restructuring the arrangement to optimize its effectiveness or suggesting another arrangement, such as a period of unpaid leave to be followed by a return to a conventional work arrangement.

Monitoring Impacts and Side-effects

The manager and employee will need to keep track of the performance measures they decided to apply when the arrangement was set up. They should try not to establish productivity expectations that are higher for FWA employees than for others, or to add an extra burden of record keeping to these employees' jobs.

Some arrangements are requested to make it easier for the employee to deal with existing responsibilities and involvements. Others are requested because of changes in the employee's personal responsibilities. In the latter case, it is important to separate changes in the employee's work performance that are attributable to the new arrangement from changes that are attributable to having a greater burden of responsibility at home. For example, 'invisible' and unpaid extra work the employee had been doing under the old arrangement may not be possible to do when demands at home increase. The employee may no longer be able to stay late or work on weekends to finish tasks.

***Box 3.4**   Self-Management Skills*

Self-management skills are important for employees who request a new schedule that will involve longer periods of work without access to their manager and perhaps removed from co-workers. Although occasionally, co-workers distract us from our work, they also provide help and feedback at timely moments, create a motivating work atmosphere, and provide short periods of respite from work that help counteract tedium and fatigue.

Employees who work alone or outside regular hours need to plan ahead to make sure they can manage the tasks that are usually performed by others (e.g. photocopying, fixing the photocopier when it jams, changing a printer cartridge, completing forms, using computer software packages).

Self-management Skills of Telecommuters

Self-management skills are particularly important for employees who opt for telecommuting or work-at-home arrangements. This is partly because we are used to family and domestic tasks taking first priority when we are at home. It is common for those working at home to take short breaks to accomplish household tasks. These breaks can function in much the same way that workplace breaks do, by providing short, distracting rest periods. However, the length of these breaks needs to be controlled, just as they would in the workplace. Although there may be one or two specific house-hold or caregiving tasks that require their attention for a short period, employees who work at home should not commit themselves to completing major household chores by the end of the day. If the employee had to go to the worksite, everything at home would be in exactly the same state at the end of the day as it was at the beginning, and the dinner would not be ready. These same expectations should also apply to a work-at-home situation.

Given the diversions and opportunities for relaxation that one's home can offer, prospective telecommuters will need to determine whether the temptations to read, to watch TV, to sleep in or to go out shopping are likely to interfere with the demands and deadlines of their jobs. In addition, some individuals would find working alone at home lonely and dull, compared to the dialogue, stimulation, and support often provided by workplace relationships. In short, work-at-home arrangements are not suitable for every employee, and therefore particular care should be taken to monitor employees' satisfaction and productivity in these situations.

Children at Home

The most difficult situation to manage is working at home when family dependents are present. The reality is that most job tasks require concentrated and sustained attention, and therefore cannot be efficiently accomplished if they are frequently interrupted. Thus, to work at the same level of productivity as an average employee who is in the workplace, telecommuters who work at home cannot be responsible for caring for family members, especially young children. Employees who plan to work at home while their children are there need to have someone else take responsibility for the children, and they need a clearly defined work area (a study, office, workshop, or studio) with a door that can be closed. Taking the children to a local daycare centre or babysitter during working hours is another solution.

(continued)

Adult Family Members at Home

Adult family members may also disrupt the employee who wishes to work at home. A spouse, an elderly parent who lives with the employee, or family or friends who know that the employee is home may need to be told that chats, phone calls, or errands have to be deferred to break times. Thus, an employee who plans to work at home has to set some clear ground rules for themselves and other family members and friends about times when he or she will be working, times for breaks, and the types of interruptions that are and are not acceptable during work periods.

Start and Finish Times

Employees who are working alone in the workplace or who are working at home should also track their hours so that there is a point in the day when it is 'quitting time'. It is psychologically important to know when a full day's work has been completed, and when work can be set aside in good conscience.

During the initial period after the FWA is implemented, schedule a few meetings (at the end of the first week and at the end of the first month) to discuss how the arrangement is working out. This provides an opportunity to remedy quickly any problems that have a negative impact on productivity, including difficulties communicating and coordinating with co-workers.

Poor cooperation from other workers can have a variety of causes. The most aggravating problem is when burdensome extra tasks are transferred to co-workers to accommodate the FWA user, without any compensation or even recognition for the extra work or responsibility they assume. Other reasons for a chilled relationship between FWA users and their co-workers include envy of the arrangements on the part of employees who have been deemed ineligible to use them, a sense of inequity because co-workers did not have an opportunity to use such an arrangement when they needed it in the past, or resentment toward a manager who is perceived to grant preferential treatment to this employee.

Employees and their managers should be sure they ask co-workers and any subordinates how the new arrangement is affecting them. When co-workers and subordinates can voice their feelings or concerns, it is easier to respond appropriately.

Fine-tuning FWAs

For the most part, both employees who are using FWAs and their managers report no adverse effect of the arrangements on employees' workplace performance (see Chapter Four for more details). In terms of work–family balance, morale, and general well-being, however, the benefits for the employee are usually appreciable. Job performance certainly can be affected, however, so the employee and the manager should meet at the end of the trial period to review any productivity information they can rely on. Other, less tangible impacts should also be discussed, including any effects of the change in schedule on the employee's job-related stress, relationships with co-workers, satisfaction with job responsibilities, and prospects for career advancement.

In addition to the workplace evaluation conducted with the manager, the employee should also make the effort to conduct a personal audit of the effects of the new FWA on the home front. Employees need to watch out for situations where greater flexibility in job hours results in an even heavier burden of domestic tasks. Flexibility in work hours can help improve the efficiency of the employee's time use, but cannot solve a problem stemming from role overload at home. When a long-term family responsibility cannot be managed by rescheduling or even cutting back on the hours of work, it is time to consider a personal leave.

CREATING A HOSPITABLE ORGANIZATIONAL CLIMATE

When introducing flexible work arrangements, it is essential to gain the cooperation and support of everyone involved, from senior managers to co-workers and subordinates. Without sanctions from the highest echelons, efforts to introduce and sustain these arrangements will be threatened. To achieve such support, there must be changes in some of the basic assumptions made by managers and employees about how work gets done. Specifically, as detailed in Chapter Five, management training should not only address the business case for FWAs and ways of creatively deploying personnel, but should also spur managers to reconsider their views about the relationship between work and family, notably that family problems should be left at the workplace door, and about the relationship between productivity and the number of hours that employees spend at the job site under the watchful eyes of their managers. Most observers agree that truly transformational developments in the culture of the workplace are predicated upon changes in fundamental beliefs, such as the belief that 'one size fits all' when it comes to the structure and scheduling of work, and that, to be productive, employees need to be in sight and on-site and require 'over-the-shoulder' management (Olmsted & Smith, 1994).

The mindset required for flexible work arrangements is one of mutual, not individual, responsibility. When job schedules vary on an individual basis, people must start to pay attention to one another's schedules and work as a team to accomplish unit duties and responsibilities. Coverage of working times must be coordinated within the work unit so that everyone can benefit from greater flexibility most of the time, although everyone must also rotate through periods that are unpopular (e.g. the end of the day preceding a long weekend). This may also have the effect of diminishing the hierarchical distinctions between one job position and the next, because cross-training and mutual responsibility for certain tasks will increase shared knowledge, skills, and goals.

In most organizations, managers must give their consent before employees can take time off on any given day and before they can temporarily rearrange their work pattern. Saying no to employees' requests for schedule changes is not a cost-free solution, however, particularly when it is justified on the basis of impersonal (and depersonalizing) rules. It can result in resentment, unfavourable public portrayals of the manager, and reduced loyalty to the employer. It is particularly important for managers to avoid inconsistent responses to employees with and without family responsibilities.

When employees request permanent work schedule changes, they have typically given considerable thought to the proposal, and discussed its implications with others before marshalling the courage to approach their manager with the request. These are generally earnest requests that require serious and compassionate consideration on the manager's part, even if the request can not be met in full or in the immediate future. Managers and their employees need to acknowledge and validate one another's concerns, and then engage in a dialogue about how the proposed arrangement could be modified to become more acceptable. For example, the parties must squarely address managers' apprehension that employees will be unable to keep up with their job responsibilities, or that tasks involving coordination with other workers will suffer delays. Similarly, they must confer in earnest about how the proposed arrangement will affect the employees' ability to achieve a healthy balance between their work and home life. Airing these issues and concerns, identifying ways of monitoring the new arrangement and reconvening to fine-tune it, and making advance contingency plans for problems that are more likely to arise, are all elements of a process that reflects both parties' commitment to making the new arrangement serve both personal and organizational needs.

Finally, it is essential to underscore the value of a process of negotiation, decision-making, and evaluation that reflects shared responsibility between employees and managers for the success of flexible work arrangements. It is equally important to spotlight the need for these two parties to reciprocate flexible attitudes and conduct. Whereas managers are prepared to give employees more discretion in making their own decisions about how to structure and complete their jobs, employees must be prepared to demonstrate the flexibility required to perform their duties in a manner that is responsive to the competitive pressures, market demands, and efficiency requirements in which the organization operates. To the extent that both parties live up to the terms of this reciprocal arrangement, they will nurture a climate of fairness and mutual responsiveness that will benefit employer and employee alike.

4

The Effects of Flexible Work Arrangements

As has been evident in the preceding discussion, organizations introduce flexible work arrangements for a variety of reasons. For example, they may introduce flexible work arrangements to reduce costs, absenteeism and turnover, to improve productivity and morale, or to help employees balance work and family demands. This chapter addresses the effectiveness of flexible work arrangements in achieving this diverse set of goals.

Our conclusions are based on both the published research literature and data we collected in three studies we designed as members of the Canadian Aging Research Network (CARNET). The majority of the published empirical literature focuses on two types of flexible work arrangements, namely flexitime and compressed work weeks. However, we examined the effects of a wider range of flexible work arrangements, and also answered more specific questions about the use and effectiveness of each type of work arrangement.

In particular, we draw data from three studies conducted by CARNET. First, in 1993, CARNET conducted the *Work and Family Survey*. Participants ($N = 5496$) were drawn from eight Canadian organizations representing five employment sectors: government, education, financial services, health care, and manufacturing. Second, in 1994, CARNET conducted the *Work and Home Life Survey* among 1700 employees from three Canadian organizations. Compared with the previous survey, it offered more details about participants' work and homelife responsibilities, and about employees' desire for, use, and self-rated effectiveness of flexible work arrangements.

Finally, the *Workplace Flexibility Study* was conducted in 1995. In brief, this study was an in-depth evaluation of flexible work arrangements in a large Canadian financial institution. Although limited to one corporation, the study gauged both employees' and managers' evaluations of flexible work arrangements, and therefore yielded a more informative and balanced assessment of the effectiveness of such work arrangements (the study design is detailed in Appendix A).

The goals of this chapter are threefold. First, we present information about employees' participation in flexible work arrangements, profiling the characteristics of the users of each type of arrangement. Second, we review the data addressing the effectiveness of flexible work arrangements, documenting their impact upon a variety of dimensions including productivity, employee morale, employee stress and well-being and employees' ability to harmonize their work and family demands. Third, we address a number of concerns that managers and employees express regarding potential adverse effects of flexible work arrangements on their jobs and personal lives.

WHO USES FLEXIBLE WORK ARRANGEMENTS?

Our first observation is that only a segment of the workforce needs or wants a flexible work arrangement. Moreover, employees with different personal characteristics may desire different types of flexible work arrangements. For example, individuals with many family responsibilities may prefer to reduce the number of hours spent in the workplace, whereas employees in urban areas may wish to reduce their commuting time by adopting a flexible hours or telecommuting arrangement.

Such differences in employee preferences also make it difficult to evaluate the impact of flexible work arrangements on work-related and personal outcomes. Comparisons among groups of employees using different work arrangements are made more difficult when these individuals also differ in terms of demographic characteristics, personal attributes, job position, and family responsibilities.

Table 4.1 presents a comparison of the number and demographic characteristics of six groups of respondents to the *Work and Family Survey*, namely employees who have 'normal' full-time hours, those who work flexible hours (flexitime), compressed work weeks, telecommuters, and employees who have part-time hours and job sharing. Several noteworthy differences among these groups bear spotlighting.

First, after the two 'conventional' arrangements (full-time and part-time hours), flexitime is the most prevalent of the flexible work arrangements, with just under 10% of all survey respondents working in a flexitime arrangement. Telecommuting is the next most prevalent arrangement (2.4% of all respondents), with compressed work weeks and job sharing arrangements being used by only a miniscule number of individuals (each less than 1% of all respondents).

Second, flexitime workers and employees engaged in telecommuting tend to be older, earn a higher annual salary but have less years of service than 'normal' full-time workers. Equally important, telecommuters also work substantially longer weeks ($M = 47.44$ hours) compared to full-time ($M = 43.51$ hours) or flexitime ($M = 43.41$ hours) employees.

Third, although just under 60% of full-time employees were women, approximately 80% of those using flexitime, and of those who had a compressed work week, and 92% of part-time workers were women. That is, compared to full-time workers, women are disproportionately over-represented in every alternative work arrangement except telecommuting. Conversely, women are under-represented among the telecommuters, comprising just 45% of this group. Finally, although the vast majority of all respondents reported being married or living as married, parents were somewhat over-represented among the part-time employees and under-represented among individuals working compressed work weeks.

Similar patterns emerged in the *Work and Home Life Survey* (see Table 4.2). Once again, flexitime was the most prevalent work arrangement (12.7% of all respondents) after full-time and part-time work. Relatively few individuals (approximately 2–3% of all respondents) reported working compressed work weeks, telecommuting or job sharing.

As in the *Work and Family Survey*, telecommuters and flexitime

Table 4.1 Demographic characteristics by work arrangement: Work and Family Survey

	Full time	Flexitime	Compressed work week	Telecommute	Part time	Job share
1. Number of respondents	4132	536	35	132	609	52
2. Hours/week	43.51	43.41	38.43	47.44	33.81	42.98
3. Organizational tenure (years)	13.74	10.59	13.60	10.66	10.68	13.79
4. Salary ($1000/year)	30–39	40–49	30–39	40–49	20–29	30–39
5. Age	39.94	43.41	38.43	43.04	42.10	42.10
7. Percentage with children under age 18	45.16	49.62	37.14	47.72	59.93	40.38
8. Percentage married	82.07	78.92	80.00	85.60	85.05	67.31
9. Percentage women	59.66	78.92	80.00	44.70	92.45	67.30

Table 4.2 Demographic characteristics by work arrangement: Work and Homelife Survey

	Full time	Flexitime	Compressed work week	Telecommute	Part time	Job share
1. Number of respondents	937	224	34	45	490	41
2. Hours/week	39.25	41.52	34.29	43.53	35.01	30.30
3. Organizational tenure (years)	12.94	9.26	9.64	10.48	8.61	10.48
4. Salary ($1000/year)	30–39	20–29	30–39	40–49	10–19	10–19
5. Age	42.74	39.17	38.91	42.00	40.34	36.50
6. Percentage with children under age 18	49.40	59.82	50.00	67.67	58.57	53.66
7. Percent married	76.41	72.76	65.71	95.56	77.96	65.86
8. Percentage women	59.34	66.96	60.00	48.89	89.80	63.41

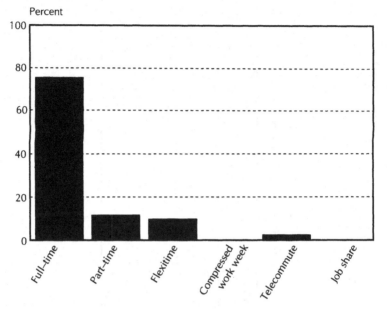

Figure 4.1   *Use of FWAs: W & F Survey*

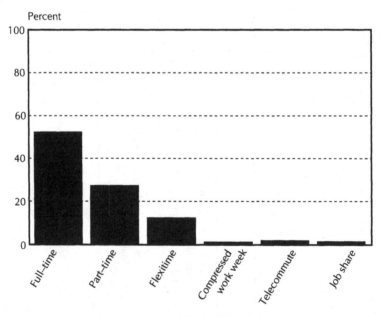

Figure 4.2   *Use of FWAs: W & H Survey*

workers reported less organizational tenure than did full-time workers. Telecommuters also reported a longer work-week and a higher annual salary than did full-time employees. Women were disproportionately over-represented among the part-time workers and somewhat more likely than men to have flexitime arrangements. Conversely, women were under-represented again in the group of telecommuters. Married individuals were over-represented in the group of telecommuters, and parents were disproportionately likely to use flexitime, telecommuting, and part-time work arrangements.

Table 4.3 presents comparable data drawn from the *Workplace Flexibility Study*. Because of the design of the study (see Appendix A), comparison of the number of workers in each work arrangement is not appropriate. However, many trends similar to those previously described can be discerned. Telecommuters tend to work longer work weeks and report higher annual salaries than do full-time employees. Flexitime workers report less organizational tenure, and telecommuters more organizational tenure, than full-time workers. Finally, although women comprise approximately 90% of the sample, they are over-represented among the part-time workers (97%) and under-represented among the telecommuters (78.3%).

Summary: Who Uses Flexible Work Arrangements?

The distribution of work arrangements and demographic characteristics of users in the three CARNET studies suggests several conclusions. First, the vast majority of employees do not have a flexible work arrangement but have conventional full-time and part-time work arrangements. Second, flexitime and telecommuting seem to be the most widely used work arrangements, with job sharing and compressed work weeks being used by a relatively small number of employees.

Third, and most importantly for our purposes, there are many demographic differences between the users of different types of work arrangements. Users of different arrangements vary in terms of their organizational position (e.g. salary, tenure), personal characteristics (e.g. sex) and family responsibilities (e.g. marital status, number of children). Therefore, any assessment of

Table 4.3 Demographic characteristics by work arrangement: Workplace Flexibility Study

	Full time	Full time (with flex)	Compressed work week	Telecommute	Part time	Part time with flex	Job share
1. Number of respondents	68	60	25	23	35	44	32
2. Hours/week (Job)	41.2	40.5	39.9	42.4	28.0	26.7	22.0
3. Organizational tenure (years)	14.6	12.6	15.2	17.4	11.4	9.2	12.6
4. Salary ($1000/year)	20–30	20–30	20–30	30–40	15–19	15–19	10–15
5. Age	38.3	38.5	38.7	40.6	37.8	34.4	37.6
7. Hours/week (Childcare)	17.0	16.0	16.1	14.6	25.6	34.8	34.8
8. Percentage women	89.7	90.0	92.0	78.3	97.1	93.2	96.9

the impact of flexible work arrangements should recognize and control for these differences.

Finally, these data raise a number of provocative questions. For example, why are women over-represented in some work arrangements (e.g. flexitime) but under-represented in others (e.g. telecommuting)? Quite possibly this finding is an outcome of the gender stratification of the workforce. That is, women are more likely to be represented in service occupations that may require direct face-to-face contact with organizational clients. As a result, these occupations may be excluded from telecommuting or work-at-home arrangements. Conversely, women may be under-represented in managerial occupations for which tele-commuting (but not job sharing) arrangements are seen as appropriate.

A more puzzling finding is that individuals who telecommute actually work longer work weeks than those who do not. Al-though this finding may reflect the nature of the individual's position and job description (e.g. managers tend to work longer work weeks than do non-managerial employees), it also suggests that telecommuters have a difficult time managing the bound-aries between their job and home lives, committing excess hours to the former domain.

THE EFFECTS OF FLEXIBLE WORK ARRANGEMENTS

Although a great deal of research has been conducted on the effectiveness of flexible work arrangements, several investiga-tors have suggested that the evidence is, at best, inconclusive (e.g. Buckley, Kicza & Crane, 1987; McGuire & Liro, 1987). In large part, their conclusion stems from the lack of rigorous evalu-ation of the impacts of flexible work arrangements. Reviews of the early research on flexitime (Golembiewski & Proehl, 1978; 1980) have been almost uniformly positive with respect to em-ployee attitudes and productivity. Unfortunately, many of these studies lack methodological rigour. Frequently, evaluations of flexitime rely solely on anecdotal evidence with no 'hard' data or statistical analysis. For example, instead of assessing job per-formance, researchers have asked employees whether they thought their performance had improved after switching to the new work arrangement. As noted in Chapter Three, the resulting data may say more about employees' desire to retain flexible work arrangements than about the true effects of such work arrangements on performance.

Moreover, such reports frequently fail to include controls for differences among people choosing a particular flexible work arrangement. Without statistical controls or the inclusion of an appropriate control group, it is difficult to determine whether any productivity gains associated with flexible work arrangements are actually attributable to the arrangement itself rather than to the characteristics of the individuals who opt for the new arrangement. For example, simple comparisons of productivity between telecommuters and non-telecommuters may not take into account the fact that telecommuters are typically more senior, and hence more experienced, employees.

More recent studies of flexible work arrangements have attempted to overcome these shortcomings by conducting field experiments and rigorous evaluations, using both longitudinal designs and multivariate statistical analyses. Although more rigorous in design, these studies have still not resolved debates about the effectiveness of flexible work arrangements. Indeed, in their review of research on flexitime, Buckley et al. (1987) appropriately observed that reports of programme success can be invariably matched with reports of flexitime failure. Although these authors were referring specifically to flexitime programmes, their observation applies equally well to the broader domain of flexible work arrangements.

In addition to the weak design of evaluation studies, there are several other reasons why evidence regarding the effectiveness of flexible work arrangements is mixed. In particular, it is conceivable that individuals who have been given the opportunity to tailor a work arrangement to their own needs and lifestyle experience better outcomes, whereas those who have been assigned to their work arrangement, even if it is defined as a flexible arrangement, experience worse outcomes. Although flexible work arrangements imply greater flexibility for the employee, true and meaningful flexibility may depend on employees choosing the work arrangements that are best suited to their circumstances. Hence, in evaluating the impacts of flexible work arrangements, one should first establish whether or not the arrangement was chosen by the employee, and only then inquire into its effects on morale, productivity, and job–family balance. As the data we present later reveal, the latter outcomes are strongly affected by taking the issue of choice of arrangement into account.

A logical starting place for assessing the effectiveness of flexible work arrangements is to consider the goals or outcomes such arrangements are intended to achieve. Many of the flexible arrangements we have considered were initially introduced to achieve a limited set of outcomes. For example, the introduction of flexitime is usually attributed to attempts in Europe to decrease traffic congestion and commuting time (e.g. Coltrin & Barendse, 1981). Currently, arrangements such as flexitime, compressed work weeks, and telecommuting are more frequently identified as 'work–family programmes' (e.g. Solomon, 1994), and therefore examine such outcomes as the degree of conflict between work and family and family role performance.

Contemporary proponents of flexible work arrangements tend to cite a wide array of potential impacts of their use. For example, Ronen (1981) enumerated the following benefits of flexitime: (a) accommodating one's own biological clock; (b) reducing the pressure of arriving at work at a specific time; (c) avoiding transportation difficulties; (d) encouraging teamwork; and (e) accommodating family responsibilities. Coltrin and Barendse (1981) offered a more extensive list of benefits, including less tardiness and absenteeism, less overtime, improved morale, increased productivity, lower turnover, improved planning and communication, less commuting time, improved customer service, broader work opportunities, and better utilization of resources.

It is difficult to imagine any organizational intervention that would have such a far-reaching impact. Most of the available research on flexible work arrangements has focussed on four types of outcomes: effects on organizational productivity, effects on employees' ability to maintain balance between their work and family responsibilities, effects on employees' stress, and effects on employees' job attitudes and morale (Dunham, Pierce & Castaneda, 1987).

Effects on Organizational Productivity

Researchers have examined the effects of flexible work arrangements on organizational productivity, using various indicators of job performance as well as records of absenteeism and tardiness. Once again, the available evidence regarding the effects of flexible work arrangements on productivity is quite mixed.

Both Orpen (1981) and Kim & Campagna (1981) reported negligible effects of flexitime on productivity. Ronen and Primps (1980) reviewed the implementation of flexitime in 25 public agencies and found varied reports of increased productivity. However, these authors also noted that there were no reports of productivity decline attributable to the implementation of flexitime, suggesting that, although flexible work arrangements may not enhance productivity, they also do not detract from productivity. Harrick, Vanek & Michlitsch (1986) report a field experiment that combined flexitime and compressed work weeks. Over a 16 month period, they report that there was no overall effect on job performance. However, Harrick, Vanek & Michlitsch (1986) also noted that there was a reduction in both sick leave and annual leave rates associated with having an alternative work schedule. Similarly, Kim & Campagna (1981) found reductions in absence rates attributable to the introduction of flexitime.

Several studies have also investigated the effects of compressed work weeks on organizational productivity. Whereas some studies have noted increases in performance (e.g. Hartman & Weaver, 1977), the more common observation has been no change in productivity (Calvasina & Boxx, 1975) after moving to a compressed work week. In an interesting series of investigations Ivancevich (1974) reported an increase in performance one year after the introduction of a compressed work week schedule. However, 24 months after the introduction of the new schedule, the effect disappeared (Ivancevich & Lyon, 1977).

Although worker productivity is frequently advanced as the rationale for adopting part-time work schedules (Barling & Gallagher, 1996), there is little empirical evidence to suggest that part-time workers are any more or less productive than full-time workers. Some researchers have reported marginal increases in productivity attributable to part-time work (e.g. Leighton, 1991; Wotruba, 1990). Other researchers have found no such increases (e.g. Jackofsky & Peters, 1987; Nollen, Eddy, Hinder & Martin, 1978).

One early review suggested that part-time workers were absent from work less often than full-time workers (Nollen, Eddy, & Hinder Martin, 1978), but this conclusion has also been subsequently challenged. For example, Smulders (1993) found that absenteeism differences between part-time and full-time workers stemmed from the type of work performed (i.e. production or non-production; shift-work or not) rather than the employment status of the individual.

Using data from the *Workplace Flexibility Study*, we compared the job performance and absenteeism of employees using a variety of flexible work arrangements. In particular, the design of the study allowed us to obtain both self-ratings and managers' ratings of performance for each employee. This is an important design consideration because there is some evidence that employees' and supervisors' ratings of employee performance rarely agree (e.g. Harris & Schaubroeck, 1988).

Results of our comparisons of productivity across the seven work arrangements are presented in Table 4.4. After statistically controlling for demographic differences between the groups of employees, there were no significant differences between employees in flexible work arrangements and employees in conventional arrangements.

Generally, these results are in substantial agreement with the published literature on flexible work arrangements. Although there does not seem to be convincing evidence that work arrangements enhance individual productivity, there is also no evidence to suggest that such arrangements inhibit or detract from productivity. In short, without taking into regard whether or not employees were in arrangements of their own choice, flexible work arrangements, in and of themselves, had little effect on productivity. We will return to this subject later, examining how productivity is affected when employees' choice of a particular arrangement is taken into account.

Table 4.4 *Effects on productivity: Workplace Flexibility Study*

	Full time	Full time (with flex)	Compressed work week	Telecommute	Part time	Part time with flex	Job share
1. Job performance							
Self rating	5.59	5.76	5.47	5.47	5.74	5.67	5.72
Supervisor rating	5.61	5.56	5.75	5.60	5.36	5.22	5.75
2. Relations with co-workers							
Self rating	5.53	5.51	5.81	5.39	5.46	5.33	5.72
Supervisor rating	5.53	5.28	5.37	5.12	5.23	5.27	5.73
3. Relations with manager							
Self rating	5.22	5.36	5.57	5.52	5.16	4.94	5.47
Supervisor rating	5.44	5.48	5.49	5.56	4.95	5.14	5.51
4. Customer service							
Self rating	6.21	6.45	6.32	6.39	6.47	6.29	6.30
Supervisor rating	5.80	6.03	5.87	5.85	5.84	5.58	5.97
5. Absenteeism (self)	2.36	2.33	2.92	1.48	1.31	1.09	1.28
6. Work interruptions (self)	1.59	1.75	3.04	2.73	0.77	0.71	0.81
7. Absenteeism (manager)	2.50	2.13	2.94	2.31	2.17	2.39	2.60
8. Work interruptions (manager)	2.35	2.11	2.53	1.67	2.05	2.19	1.87

Note: No differences are statistically significant. Managers' and subordinates' reports of absenteeism are measured using different response scales and are not directly comparable. With the exception of self-reports of absenteeism and work interruptions, scores can range from one to seven, with higher scores indicating more of the variable.

Effects on Work–Family Balance

Flexible work arrangements are frequently cited as a means of helping employees balance work and family responsibilities (e.g. Friedman, 1994; Solomon, 1994). In one of the few studies to examine this question directly, Hicks and Klimoski (1981) reported that employees who had a flexitime arrangement reported less work–family conflict than did employees who had conventional arrangements. Similarly, Barling and Barenburg (1984) found that employed mothers who had flexitime arrangements reported less work–family conflict than did employed mothers who had a regular full-time schedule.

The data from the three CARNET studies allowed us to directly examine the impact of various work arrangements on employees' ability to balance work and family involvements. To do so, we relied on employees' self-reports of the extent to which work interfered with family and family interfered with work. Again, because of demographic differences between individuals in different work arrangements, we compared individuals working in different work arrangements after statistically controlling for these variables.

The results of these comparisons are presented in Table 4.5. In both the *Work and Family Survey* and the *Work and Home Life Survey*, no significant differences were found between the groups of employees on either variable. However, data gained from the *Workplace Flexibility Study* revealed one significant difference. Employees who worked fewer than 35 hours per week reported less work interference with family than did employees who worked 35 hours per week or more.

In all three studies, no differences in work–family conflict were attributable to working flexitime or telecommuting, the two flexible work arrangements most frequently proposed to reduce work–family conflict. Moreover, in each study, those employees who were involved in work-at-home or telecommuting arrangements actually reported higher levels of work interference with family than employees who had regular, full-time schedules. Although these differences were not statistically significant, the higher degree of work–family conflict reported by telecommuters is potentially attributable to their working a longer work

Table 4.5 *Effects on Work and Family Balance*

	Full time	Full time (with flex)	Compressed work week	Telecommute	Part time	Part time with flex	Job share
Work and Family Study							
1. Work interference with family	2.58	2.55	2.47	2.66	2.54	—	2.69
2. Family interference with work	1.90	1.91	1.91	1.92	1.86	—	1.97
Work and Home Life Study							
3. Work interference with family	1.81	1.82	1.83	1.85	1.91	—	1.91
4. Family interference with work	1.47	1.47	1.49	1.51	1.50	—	1.50
Workplace Flexibility Study							
5. Work interference with family*	3.51	3.66	2.98	4.11	3.19	2.39	2.08
6. Family interference with work	2.63	2.65	2.18	2.37	2.50	2.20	2.00

Note: * Indicates a variable with a statistically significant difference.

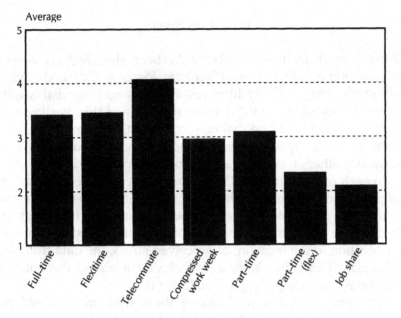

Figure 4.3 *Work interference with family: Work Flexibility Study*

week compared with employees in other arrangements (see Tables 4.1–4.3).

Although they do not imply that flexitime and telecommuting are detrimental to work–family balance, these findings belie the claim that flexitime and telecommuting facilitate improved work–family balance. Instead, they suggest that simply implementing these arrangements does not reduce the conflict employees experience between these roles.

In contrast, arrangements that involve a reduced number of hours at work are associated with lower levels of work–family conflict. Thus, individuals engaged in part-time work (with or without flexitime), job sharing and, to a lesser extent, compressed work weeks reported lower levels of work–family interference. Taken together, these observations suggest a limited effect of flexible work arrangements on work and family balance. Where such effects exist, the available data suggest that it is the absolute number of hours spent each week at work, rather than the scheduling of those hours or physical location of the employee, that is important in alleviating the cross-pressures between the job and other personal commitments.

Effects on Stress

Flexible work arrangements have also been identified as a means of reducing employee stress (Dunham, Pierce & Castaneda, 1987) although comparatively little research has addressed this outcome. In one of the few studies that examined this, Barling and Barenburg (1984) found that employed mothers working a flexitime schedule reported less depressed behaviour than did employed mothers working a standard, full-time schedule.

In each of the three CARNET studies, we included a measure of self-reported stress. Although the actual measures varied across the three studies, each one assessed the frequency of occurrence of common symptoms of stress in the last six months. In addition to the measure of perceived stress, the data from the *Workplace Flexibility Study* also included a global measure of personal well-being (i.e. life satisfaction).

In each study, our analyses of these measures yielded no significant differences between groups on the stress measure. In the *Workplace Flexibility Study*, we did find a difference between groups on the measure of personal well-being. Individuals working in reduced hours arrangements (i.e. part-time and job sharing) reported a higher level of personal well-being than individuals working in a full-time work arrangement (see Table 4.6).

Again, these data suggest a limited role of flexible work arrangements in reducing employee stress. Part-time workers and individuals engaged in job sharing reported greater life satisfaction, possibly as a result of lower levels of work–family conflict (see Figure 4.3).

Effects on Employee Attitudes and Morale

Researchers have also addressed the effects of flexible work arrangements on employee morale and attitudes toward the job and the organization. Attitudinal changes resulting from flexible work arrangements have been among the most frequently studied outcomes. Although the findings are variable, there is some evidence to suggest that the implementation of flexible work arrangements has some positive effects on employee attitudes.

Table 4.6 *Effects on employee stress*

	Full time	Full time (with flex)	Compressed work week	Telecommute	Part time	Part time (with flex)	Job share
Work and Family Study							
1. Stress	2.34	2.41	2.29	2.44	2.39	—	2.37
Work and Home Life Survey							
2. Stress	2.67	2.61	2.60	2.46	2.59	—	2.62
Workplace Flexibility Study							
3. Stress	3.90	4.08	3.72	3.92	3.37	3.38	3.14
4. Personal well-being*	4.04	3.95	4.61	4.19	4.80	5.23	5.83

Note: * Indicates a statistically significant difference. Scores can range from one to seven. Higher scores indicate more of the variable.

Notably, a meta-analysis by Neuman, Edwards & Raju (1989) reported moderate effects of flexitime and compressed work weeks on employee attitudes. A meta-analysis is based on combining research results from a number of studies. Therefore, the results reported by Neuman et al. (1989) are striking because they suggest that, across studies, flexible work arrangements exercise a measurable impact on employee attitudes.

Despite this general conclusion, the effect of such interventions on overall job satisfaction is quite mixed. For example, Orpen's (1981) field study of the introduction of flexible work hours found increases in employee satisfaction as a result of the intervention. In a similar study, Hicks and Klimoski (1981) found no differences in satisfaction.

Researchers have also considered more specific attitudes than overall job satisfaction. These studies have generally led to more positive conclusions. For example, McGuire and Liro (1987) found no differences in employee job satisfaction attributable to flexitime, but did find that flexitime workers were more satisfied with their work environment and were more willing to continue with their current work schedules than were other employees. Similarly, Harrick et al. (1986) reported that workers who adopted a flexitime arrangement reported more satisfaction with their work schedule than did other employees. Once again, there were no differences in overall employee job satisfaction.

Considerable research has addressed attitudinal differences between part-time and full-time workers. As Barling and Gallagher (1996) point out, these studies have reached every possible conclusion; i.e. part-time workers are *less* satisfied with their jobs than full-time workers; part-time workers are *more* satisfied with their jobs than full-time workers; and there are *no significant differences* between part-time and full-time workers. Generally, studies that have statistically controlled for demographic differences between part-time and full-time employees have reported no differences in employee satisfaction. This observation suggests that any effect of part-time work on employee satisfaction is attributable to the demographic characteristics of part-time employees or to the nature of the jobs they perform, rather than to the part-time schedule itself.

In each of the three CARNET surveys we asked employees to rate their overall satisfaction with the job. In the *Work and Home life Survey* we also obtained measures of employees' commitment to the company and intent to seek a new job at another company. Narayanan and Nath (1982) suggested that the effects of flexible work arrangements could be attributable to better supervisory relations obtained under such arrangements rather than to the arrangements themselves. In the *Workplace Flexibility Study*, measures of managerial, co-worker, and organizational support, as well as job satisfaction, were included. Additionally, employees were asked about their intentions to seek another job either with their current employer (internal turnover) or with another employer (external turnover).

Results of these analyses are presented in Table 4.7 and were variable across the three studies. In the *Work and Family Survey*, respondents who were working in telecommuting and part-time work arrangements reported higher levels of overall satisfaction with their jobs. In the *Work and Home Life Survey*, there were no significant differences in job satisfaction, but telecommuters reported higher commitment to the organization. Correspondingly, both telecommuters and part-time employees reported lower intentions to seek a new job.

In the *Workplace Flexibility Study*, employees working in flexitime, compressed work week and job sharing arrangements reported higher satisfaction with their jobs than did employees in other types of work arrangements. Conversely, employees working part-time (without flexitime) saw the organization as less supportive than did employees working in other arrangements.

In sum, these findings suggest some modest, positive effects of flexible work arrangements on employee attitudes and morale. However, these effects seem to be variable across setting and possibly dependent on the type of morale measures chosen. Across our three CARNET surveys, we found an effect of flexible work arrangements on job satisfaction in two of the three studies. However, the effect was not consistent, with different groups of employees reporting higher levels of job satisfaction in each study.

Table 4.7 *Effects on Employee Morale*

	Full time	Full time (with flex)	Compressed work week	Telecommute	Part time	Part time (with flex)	Job share
Work and Family Study							
1. Job satisfaction	3.72	3.69	3.77	3.92	3.90	—	3.80
Work and Home Life Study							
2. Job satisfaction	3.53	3.67	3.58	3.61	3.60	—	3.63
3. Intent to turnover	3.81	3.85	3.94	3.66	3.64	—	3.91
Workplace Flexibility Study							
4. Job satisfaction	4.07	4.52	5.08	4.13	4.19	3.99	4.84
5. Manager support	5.25	5.63	5.50	5.11	5.07	5.52	5.42
6. Co-worker support	5.81	6.09	6.19	5.56	5.65	5.59	5.64
7. Organizational support	4.15	3.89	4.29	3.79	3.36	3.80	4.11
8. Internal turnover	3.72	4.61	3.37	3.45	3.73	3.24	3.63
9. External turnover	2.50	2.55	2.05	2.30	2.68	2.60	2.19

Note: Scores can range from one to seven. Higher scores indicate more of the variable.

Summary: The Impact of Flexible Work Arrangements

The data reviewed thus far do not present a convincing case either for or against the implementation of flexible work arrangements. The effects of such arrangements on measures of productivity are difficult to establish. Although there is some evidence that flexible work arrangements have an impact on work–family balance and employee stress, these findings appear to be attributable to a reduction in work hours rather than alternative methods of scheduling the work. Similarly, the effects of flexible work arrangements on various measures of morale and employee attitudes seem quite variable, although there is some evidence that employees prefer flexible work arrangements to more traditional work arrangements.

Although the case these data make for implementing flexible work arrangements may seem quite weak, it is important to note that the findings do not show any negative effects of implementing flexible work arrangements. Hence, it is appropriate to conclude that flexible work arrangements are effectively neutral in terms of organizational functioning, with some potential for improving employee morale.

THE IMPACT OF CHOICE

As suggested earlier, one possible explanation for the inconsistent effects of flexible work arrangements on performance, work–family balance, stress, and attitudinal outcomes is that researchers have not taken the issue of choice of arrangement into account. After all, it is conceivable that employees who are assigned to their work arrangements do not find that it offers the flexibility or the sense of control they need or want, as compared to employees who have been given the opportunity to customize an arrangement to their own situations and lifestyles.

This suggestion is consistent with a recent evaluation of family supportive workplace polices by Thomas and Ganster (1995). Based on the responses of 398 health professionals in 45 acute care facilities, Thomas and Ganster (1995) found effects of flexible scheduling on employees' perceptions of control over their work and family concerns. In turn, these perceptions of control were related to improved employee morale (job satisfaction), decreased stress (depression, somatic complaints and blood cholesterol), and decreased work–family conflict. Importantly, flexible scheduling did not affect these outcomes directly. Rather, it affected these outcomes by increasing employees' perceptions of being in control.

Data from the *Workplace Flexibility Study* allowed us to examine how respondents entered their respective work arrangements. Specifically, we asked whether they were hired into their current work arrangement, whether their employer assigned them to their current work arrangement after they were hired, or whether they were in a work arrangement that they had personally requested. We determined that people who had been hired into or assigned to their arrangement represented the 'no choice' group, whereas those who had elected or chosen their arrangement represented the 'choice' group. We also asked respondents whether they preferred another work arrangement and, if so, which arrangement they preferred. These questions allowed us to determine whether or not employees had exercised control over the fit between their personal lives and their work arrangement.

Several enlightening empirical trends emerged from these comparisons (see Table 4.8). The majority of employees who had flexible work arrangements were either hired into or assigned their arrangement by the employer. With the exception of telecommuting (56% of those working this arrangement requested it) and job sharing (48% of job sharers requested this arrangement), it appears that most employees had little say about the work arrangement they occupied.

The issue of choice takes on even greater importance when one examines the preferred work arrangements of employees who were hired into or assigned to their arrangements. For example, 89% of employees who had a regular, full-time schedule were either hired into or assigned to this schedule. A whopping 71% of these individuals expressed a preference for another arrangement! Similarly, 75% of those working full-time with flexible hours did not request this arrangement. Over half (52%) of these employees also preferred another work arrangement. Conversely, the majority of telecommuters (56%) requested this arrange-

Table 4.8   *Type of entry into current work arrangement and preference for another arrangement*

		Type of Entry			
Current arrangement	Hired	Assigned	Self-selected	Prefer other arrangement
1. Full time	44(64%)	17(25%)	8(12%)	71%
2. Flexible hours (FT)	20(34%)	24(41%)	15(25%)	52%
3. Compressed work week	5(20%)	12(48%)	8(32%)	64%
4. Telecommuting	2(9%)	8(35%)	13(56%)	39%
5. Job sharing	5(16%)	11(35%)	15(48%)	22%
6. Part time	8(24%)	17(50%)	9(26%)	57%
7. Flexible hours (PT)	8(18%)	24(55%)	12(27%)	43%

ment, and only 39% of them expressed a desire for another work arrangement.

Overall, the majority of employees (63%) who were hired into a particular work arrangement preferred to change to a new arrangement. Just over half (52%) of those who were assigned a particular arrangement wanted to change. Only 39% of those who requested a particular arrangement wanted to change. This observation suggests that the actual work arrangement that an employee has may not be as important as the opportunity for employees to choose a work arrangement that is consistent with their individual circumstances, lifestyles, and needs.

What are the most popular work arrangements? We asked the individuals who wished to change their current arrangement to identify the arrangement they would prefer. Flexible hours (61%) and compressed work weeks (60%) were the two most popular choices. Considering the patterns of usage of flexible work arrangements presented earlier (see especially Tables 4.1 and 4.2), the popularity of flexible hours is to be expected; i.e. this is the single most prevalent 'flexible' work arrangement. The popularity of compressed work weeks was unexpected; comparatively few individuals in any of the three CARNET surveys had compressed work weeks. It is important to note that these two most popular choices are also the flexible work arrangements that would not decrease employees' income. That is, flexitime and compressed work weeks both involve working the same number of weekly hours as employees currently work. Only the schedul-

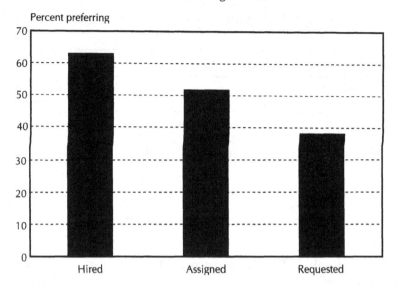

Figure 4.5   *Preference for another arrangement: Workplace Flexibility Study*

ing of those hours changes with a shift to a flexible work arrangement.

Given that most individuals are not working in their preferred work arrangement, what is the effect of being allowed to request or choose a new arrangement? To answer this question, we constructed two groups of respondents based on the data from the *Workplace Flexibility Study*. First, we identified a group of employees ($N = 42$) who reported that they had requested their current work arrangement. The second group of employees were either hired into their current work arrangement or were assigned to the arrangement by their employer ($N = 135$). We then replicated the series of analyses reported earlier. Again, because of demographic differences between the groups, we also implemented statistical controls. This allowed us to isolate the effect of choice on the various outcome measures.

Effects on Productivity

Table 4.9 presents the analysis of the effects of working a desired work arrangement on organizational variables. There was no difference in employees' performance, workplace relationships,

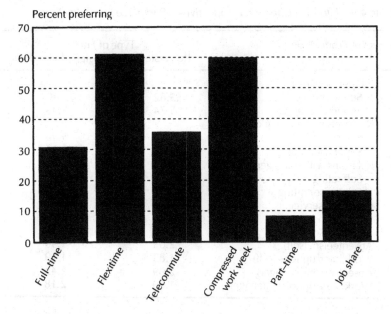

Figure 4.6 *Preference for flexible arrangements: Workplace Flexibility Study*

or absenteeism as a function of whether or not they had requested their current work arrangement. However, managers' ratings reveal a dramatically different picture (see Figure 4.7).

Managers' ratings of employees who had requested their current work arrangement reflected higher levels of job performance, better customer and co-worker relationships, and slightly better relationships with their managers than employees who were hired into or assigned to their current work arrangement. Managers also reported that employees who had requested their current work arrangement were less likely to engage in long-term (greater than three days) absenteeism. Again, employee self-reports did not reflect these differences.

This is a puzzling set of findings. The data from employees showed no differences in their job performance as a function of whether or not they had chosen their work arrangement. However, the managers' responses did reveal such differences, and in every case confirmed that employees who had opted into their current arrangement were performing at a level superior to employees who had been hired into or assigned to a particular work arrangement. It is possible that the discrepancy between

Table 4.9   *Effects of Choice on Productivity: Workplace Flexibility Study*

Aspect of Productivity	Type of Entry	
	Requested	Assigned/Hired into
1. Job performance		
Self rating	5.82	5.69
Supervisor rating	5.74	5.43
2. Relations with co-workers		
Self rating	5.52	*5.48*
Supervisor rating	5.60	5.26
3. Relations with manager		
Self rating	5.55	5.22
Supervisor rating	5.60	5.30
4. Customer service		
Self rating	6.21	6.31
Supervisor rating	6.10	5.74
5. Absenteeism (self)	2.05	1.99
6. Work interruptions (self)	1.83	1.19
7. Absenteeism (manager)	2.09	2.42
8. Work interruptions (manager)	1.89	2.18

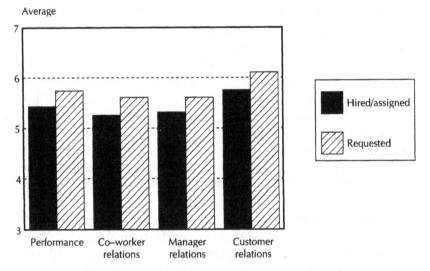

Figure 4.7   *Impact of choice on productivity: Workplace Flexibility Study*

employees' and managers' reports is a function of the two individuals using different criteria in assessing performance effectiveness. Thus, managers are more likely to focus on observable outcomes in rating performance. Employees also may include the amount of effort they are expending or the amount of difficulty they are experiencing in performing a given task in their assessment of performance.

Effects on Work–Family Balance

The effects of personally choosing a desired work arrangement on measures of work–family conflict are presented in Table 4.10. Employees who had requested their current work arrangement reported marginally less work interference with family than employees who had been hired into or assigned to their current work arrangement. There were no significant differences in family interference with work between the two groups.

These findings are not surprising. By choosing a particular work arrangement, employees presumably select a schedule or pattern that is best suited to their needs. In this case, employees are selecting the arrangement that they believe will minimize the impact of work on their family lives. They do so by structuring their work schedules in a manner that is consistent with their family responsibilities or other commitments outside work.

In contrast, it is unlikely that any form of work arrangement could affect the extent to which family interferes with work. In this case, because the interference originates in the family role, it is difficult to imagine how changing a work arrangement could affect the extent or nature of family demands.

Effects on Stress

Figure 4.8 presents the analysis in terms of employee stress and well-being. Employees who had an arrangement they requested reported lower levels of stress and higher levels of personal well-being than employees who were hired into or assigned to their current work arrangement.

Table 4.10   *Effects of Choice on Work and Family Balance: Workplace Flexibility Study*

		Type of Entry	
Aspect of productivity		Requested	Assigned/Hired into
1.	Work interference with family	2.97	3.28
2.	Family interference with work	2.43	2.40

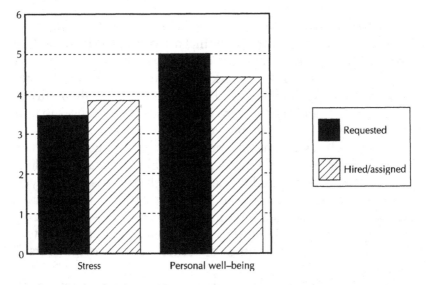

Figure 4.8   *Effects of choice on stress and well-being: Workplace Flexibility Study*

These findings are consistent with the accumulated evidence that choice and control moderate stress and boost morale (Karasek, 1979). By choosing a work arrangement that suits their personal needs and circumstances, employees experience less stress and increase their sense of well-being. It is possible that these findings also reflect the lower levels of work interference with family (i.e. one source of stress) reported by individuals who chose their current work arrangement.

Effects on Employee Attitudes and Morale

Finally, Table 4.11 presents the same comparisons for the attitudinal and morale measures. No significant differences in job satisfaction, manager's support, co-worker support, or either measure of turnover intentions emerged as a result of whether employees had requested their current work arrangement or not.

This is an interesting counterpoint to the analyses of flexible work arrangements presented earlier. The strongest effects of working under different arrangements were noted for employee attitudes and morale measures, with no effects on employee performance, stress or ability to balance work and family demands. In contrast, the ability to choose an appropriate work arrangement appears to be unrelated to morale but strongly related to performance, stress, and ability to balance work and family demands. The implication of these findings is that companies may be able to obtain all of the projected benefits by: (a) providing employees with access to a range of flexible work arrangements; and (b) allowing employees the freedom to choose the arrangement that best suits their individual needs and circumstance.

Summary: The Impact of Choice

Earlier, we concluded that there is not a compelling case to be made for the introduction of flexible work arrangements based on their effects on individual productivity, work–family balance, or stress. We also noted that the effects of flexible work arrangements on employee attitudes and morale were quite variable. We now amend this conclusion, suggesting that there is a compelling case for having employees choose flexible work arrangements. Based on the data from the *Workplace Flexibility Study*, it appears that the benefits of flexible work arrangements arise from and are contingent upon the subjective sense of enhanced control that employees gain from choosing the arrangement that is right for them.

In particular, employees who were able to choose their own

Table 4.11   *Effects of Choice on Employee Attitudes/Morale: Workplace Flexibility Study*

Aspect of productivity	Type of entry	
	Requested	Assigned/Hired into
1. Job satisfaction	4.40	4.39
2. Manager support	5.60	5.32
3. Co-worker support	5.60	5.74
4. Organizational support	3.81	3.76
5. Internal turnover	3.57	3.79
6. External turnover	2.48	2.40

work arrangements were rated higher in job performance and in customer, co-worker and manager relations than those individuals who did not choose their current arrangements. Importantly, these differences emerged based on managerial ratings of performance, thereby minimizing the possibility that employees were exaggerating their level of performance in order to retain their preferred work arrangements.

Although employees' reports of performance did not differ as a function of whether or not they had chosen their current work arrangement, they did report differences in both stress and work–family balance. Specifically, employees who had chosen their current work arrangement reported less stress, higher levels of personal well-being, and less work interference with family than those employees who had no choice in selecting their current work arrangement.

These findings are consistent with those of Thomas and Ganster (1995). It is the ability to choose an appropriate work schedule, and the resulting increase in perceived control, that appears to affect productivity, stress, and work–family balance. Hence, to optimize the personal and organizational benefits of flexible work initiatives, management should give employees the opportunity to choose the arrangements they desire, rather than assigning employees to them.

Findings from the CARNET *Work and Home Life Survey* also support the role of control. In that survey, respondents were asked directly about their perceptions of control over their time. Two interesting findings emerged. First, employees in-

	Outcome	Grade	Comment
1	Productivity	F	No observable effect
2	Work and family balance	C–	Some effects attributable to reduced hours arrangements
3	Stress	C–	Some effects attributable to reduced hours arrangements
4	Morale/attitudes	B–	Evidence for a positive effect. Results are variable across studies

Figure 4.9 *Choice of FWAs: a report card*

volved in telecommuting and flexitime reported more control over their work schedule than did employees in any other work arrangement (see Table 4.12). Second, although work arrangements were unrelated to stress and the ability of individuals to manage their work and family commitments, control perceptions were directly related to both stress and work interference with family. Employees with a greater sense of control reported less stress and less work–family conflict than did employees with a lower sense of control over their schedules. Thus, although flexible work arrangements may not, in themselves, be particularly beneficial to employees or to the organization, the enhanced sense of control that is associated with working in a flexible arrangement that one has chosen does have beneficial effects.

These observations have direct implications for the implementation of flexible work arrangements in organizations. They imply that employees should be involved in designing, implementing and evaluating their own arrangements in a manner that we have outlined in Chapter Three. Simply introducing a set of flexible work arrangement and then assigning individuals to those arrangements are unlikely to result in benefits for either the individual or the organization. Giving individual employees the option of selecting a work arrangement that suits their needs or circumstances is likely to be far more effective.

Table 4.12   *Effects of Flexible Work Arrangements on Perceptions of Control: Work and Home life Survey*

Work arrangement	Control
1. Flexible hours	4.08
2. Compressed work week	3.79
3. Telecommuting	4.73
4. Job sharing	3.78
5. Full time	3.81
6. Part time	3.73

Management Concerns

Thus far, we have focussed on the outcomes of flexible work arrangements. Now we turn our attention to concerns about the management of employees in such arrangements. Managers express a variety of concerns about having employees work flexible work arrangements. Coltrin and Barendse (1981) and Partridge (1973) identify such management concerns as the increased need for planning, increased costs, being unable to closely supervise employees who are working away from the office or outside the managers' hours, and the increased need for more flexible employees. The latter concern stems from the observation that all employees may be required to change their work habits to accommodate some employees who are involved in flexible work arrangements. Managers also express concerns about employees' availability for meetings and whether such employees can assume the same level of responsibilities as employees who have conventional schedules.

In the *Workplace Flexibility Study*, we asked managers to evaluate the effect of having employees working flexible work arrangements on eight different aspects of the managers' own job: workload; planning; costs and budgeting; workflow efficiency of the unit; planning and scheduling meetings; ability to meet branch performance goals; morale of co-workers; and the amount of responsibility that can be assigned to the employee. Managers were asked to evaluate how the employee being rated affected managers' jobs on a scale ranging from one (very negative effect) to seven (very positive effect). A rating of four reflected no effect on the managers' jobs.

As shown in Table 4.13, managers generally did not perceive any adverse effects of their employees having flexible work arrangements. Moreover, managers' ratings did not vary as a function of the type of work arrangement that the employee was in.

It is important to note that these data do not suggest that managers' concerns are unwarranted. For example, we did not address the possibility of difficulties arising during the initial 'breaking in' period, when employees commenced their use of a flexible arrangement. A better interpretation of these data is that any problems created for management are surmountable and dissipate as both managers and employees make adjustments and become accustomed to the new arrangements.

Co-worker Concerns

The co-workers of individuals who have flexible work arrangements may also be concerned about the impact of such arrangements on their own jobs. In particular, co-workers may be concerned about potential burdens that are placed on them as a result of the need to accommodate the flexible work arrangement users. For example, co-workers may be concerned about undesirable changes in the scheduling of meetings or the possibility that they will have to increase their workload to 'cover' for the employee using a flexible work arrangement. Occasionally, they have concerns about favouritism on the part of management; users of flexible work arrangements may be perceived as favoured by the supervisor, who changes meeting schedules or reallocates work to accommodate the new arrangement.

Although these concerns are certainly valid, our data show no adverse effect of flexible work arrangements on the morale of co-workers. Indeed, most individuals report that having a co-worker adopt a flexible work arrangement has little or no undesirable impact in the workplace. Moreover, a substantial minority of co-workers report that they are planning to ask for a flexible work arrangement themselves as a result of their colleagues' experience. Nonetheless, the concerns of co-workers underscore

Table 4.13 *Effect of Flexible Work Arrangements on Managers' Jobs: Workplace Flexibility Study*

	Full time	Full time (with flex)	Compressed work week	Telecommute	Part time	Part time with flex	Job share
1. My own workload	4.22	4.06	4.42	4.08	4.00	4.00	4.13
2. The planning I do	4.18	4.19	4.16	3.92	4.06	4.19	4.20
3. Costs and budgeting	4.28	4.22	4.26	4.00	4.67	4.74	4.80
4. The workflow/efficiency of my unit	4.60	4.39	4.63	4.31	4.78	4.67	4.53
5. The planning and scheduling of meetings	4.22	4.14	4.16	3.77	4.28	3.55	3.73
6. My ability to meet branch performance goals	4.50	4.53	4.79	4.46	4.33	4.42	4.80
7. The morale of co-workers	4.28	4.53	4.79	4.31	4.39	4.74	5.00
8. The amount of responsibility I can give this employee	4.60	4.78	4.68	4.77	4.33	4.10	4.13

the importance of sensitively managing the implementation of flexible work arrangements, using the steps outlined in Chapter Three.

SUMMARY AND CONCLUSIONS

Drawing on the published literature and on data from the three CARNET surveys, we have evaluated the impact of flexible work arrangements on four sets of primary outcomes: organizational productivity, employees' ability to balance work and family responsibilities, employee stress, and employee attitudes and morale. In brief, the available data suggest that flexible work arrangements have negligible effects on organizational productivity, employees' ability to balance work and family responsibilities, and stress. Although there do seem to be some improvements in employee attitudes and morale associated with these arrangements, the extent and nature of these improvements are quite variable across studies.

We also asked whether employees' ability to choose their own work arrangement had any effects on these same outcomes. The answer to this question was considerably more positive. Employees who reported choosing their current work arrangement: (a) were rated higher on performance measures by their managers; (b) reported less stress and greater personal well-being; and (c) reported less work interference with family than employees who were either hired into or assigned to their current work arrangements.

Taken together, these results suggest that the benefits of flexible work arrangements accrue primarily through increases in the sense of control gained by employees who have the opportunity to select a work arrangement that is consistent with their circumstances. This finding implies that an effective strategy for organizations is to have employees involved in both the design and selection of flexible work arrangements, a process that we describe in Chapter Three. Both our consulting experience and our empirical data suggest that such a participative approach is most likely to optimize the benefits of increased organizational productivity and enhanced personal well-being.

Appendix A
Design of the *Workplace Flexibility Study*

The *Workplace Flexibility Study* was conducted in 1995 by the Canadian Aging Research Network (CARNET). The aims of the study were to evaluate the use and effects of flexible work arrangements in a large Canadian financial institution. Employees were selected for inclusion in the study if they were identified as having a work arrangement involving either:

(a)   Flexible hours;
(b)   Job sharing;
(c)   Compressed work weeks;
(d)   Telecommuting;
(e)   Part-time hours.

In addition, a control group of employees who had standard full-time schedules were included in the study. Respondents were drawn from across the main operational areas of the organization.

To ensure an adequate representation of flexible work arrangements, all branch managers in Ontario were asked to identify employees using the work arrangements listed above. In addition, a random sample of full-time and part-time employees was drawn from organizational records.

Questionnaires were sent to each employee identified as a potential participant in the study, as well as to the managers of those employees. In total, 287 employees returned usable questionnaires for a response rate of 79%. In addition, 214 managers

(84%) returned usable questionnaires. After matching managers to their respective employees, 177 matched pairs were identified. These 177 pairs provided the data for the study.

In the employee version of the questionnaire, participants answered questions concerning morale (job satisfaction, the amount of support they received from managers, co-workers, and the organization, intention to seek a new job within the organization, intention to seek a new job outside the organization), stress (common symptoms of stress and personal well-being or life satisfaction), work–family balance (the extent to which work interfered with family and family interfered with work), and performance (quantity and quality of work, relations with co-workers, managers, customers, absence, and daily work interruptions). With the exception of the absence and work interruptions questions, all measures were taken on a response scale ranging from one to seven with higher scores representing more of the variable being measured.

Managers were asked to provide ratings of employees' job performance, customer relations, co-worker relations, and relations with management, as well as ratings of absence and work interruptions. Again, ratings ranged from one to seven with higher scores reflecting more of the variable being measured.

5

Sage Advice from Experience: On Management Training and the Implementation Process

This chapter calls on the experience of managers, employees, and human resources personnel to address optimal ways of planning and implementing flexible work arrangements. In addition, it discusses the steps that can be taken to embed flexibility in organizational policies and practices at every level, and thereby to create a culture that prizes and rewards collective flexibility as a strategy for maintaining a quality workforce and fostering its productivity and morale. Specifically, the chapter centres on the nuances entailed in:

- effectively implementing management training programmes that address flexible policies and practices;
- collaboratively planning and problem-solving around flexible work arrangements; and
- nurturing a flexible corporate culture.

GUIDELINES FOR MANAGEMENT TRAINING

There is little question that, from the employee's perspective, company policies, rewards, and sanctions are represented by and filtered through their managers or supervisors. A cardinal unwritten rule of organizational life is that an 'end run' which bypasses the formal chain of authority is tantamount to career suicide. An employee's first recourse should always be the immediate supervisor. For this reason, it is essential not only for employees to try to anticipate all the ways that a proposed flexible work arrangement might affect their managers' and co-workers' functioning, but also for managers to gain the information they need to decide whether or not to grant requests. Specifically, to comprehend the 'business case' for flexibility, managers should receive training that equips them with the knowledge, attitudes and skills needed to motivate and demonstrate their flexibility.

In addition, it will be necessary to alter the organizational culture in ways that reinforce and reward managerial flexibility. Without appropriate education, training, and discussion, managers are likely to perceive alternative work arrangements as a set of undesirable favours they must do for marginal employees who cannot cope with a conventional work arrangement, and who therefore should probably be dismissed. In addition, managers may come to resent the extra complexity and perceived loss of control involved in supervising a group that works at unusual times and even in locations where they cannot be observed. And finally, without appropriate 'buy-in', managers may refuse to grant flexible work arrangements or they may subvert them, thereby communicating to other employees that such arrangements will damage or preclude their chances for advancement. The following quotation from one bank employee reveals yet another undesirable stance that management may adopt toward flexible work arrangements, namely to convey to employees that they are a luxury which can only be afforded and awarded *after* the bank's needs are met:

> Because of the ages of my children and the failing health of my mother, I feel that demands on my time personally are stretched to the limit. My job is very demanding, with hours that are dictated by my clients' needs. This does offer me some flexibility in that I can take time off during the day to do what I need to do personally, but these hours are more than made up for in the evenings. I often put my kids to bed and come back and work until one or two a.m. My energy level is suffering and I have little time for myself or for exercise. I realize the commitment to the work and lifestyle programme on the part of my two managers. But in reality, the programme is treated as something to achieve *after* all other objectives are met at the regional level.

To optimize the likelihood of managerial 'buy-in' and strategic utilization of alternative work arrangements, it is necessary but insufficient to launch education and training sessions. In addition, senior management, including individuals at the very highest echelons of the organization, must publicly champion, model, and reward flexibility, communicating their approval of measures that promise to meet the needs of a diverse workforce while enhancing the organization's mission and business agenda. Senior management must be prepared to back up the rhetoric of flexibility by creating career paths for people who opt out of the standard mould, and by opening the ranks of leadership to those who have proved themselves on the basis of their talents rather than on the basis of their willingness to work gruelling 60 hour weeks.

EFFECTIVE STRATEGIES OF MANAGERIAL TRAINING

Managerial training programmes must be carefully designed to communicate the necessary information in the most impactful ways. Since time itself is one of the manager's most precious commodities, the training should be carefully structured according to an agenda with predetermined time limits for each item. Ideally, this agenda should be informed by input from all or a subgroup that is representative of its intended audience. For example, in advance of the training session, people can be asked to rate the extent of their knowledge about a set of topics related to workplace flexibility, or about their felt need for further education in this area. For instance, although Figure 5.1 was designed to show the results of the US Conference Board's 1992 survey of managerial knowledge and information needs regarding the intersection of work and family, it could be adapted for use as a needs assessment tool by those planning management training sessions on the subject. Such a tool could be used to customize the training content for different organizational units, depending on their perceived information needs.

Managers are more likely to respond to an assessment instrument that calls for ratings rather than open-ended responses, not only because of the time savings but also because a predesignated list of possible topics communicates to managers that the planners are well organized and well informed. Moreover, by exposing managers to a tentative list of the subjects that may be

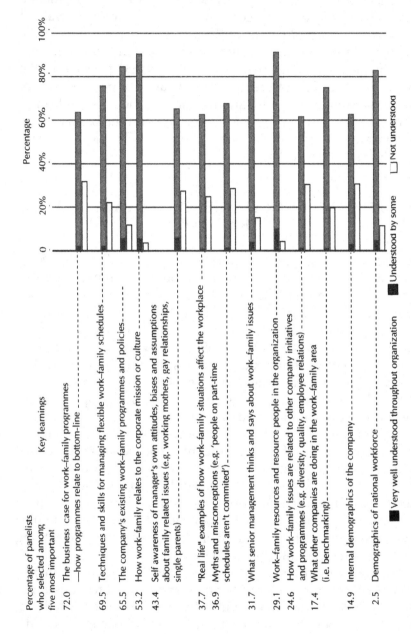

Figure 5.1 What managers need to know and how well they know it. Reproduced by permission of the Conference Board

addressed in the training session, the assessment instrument presensitizes them to these topics and previews the training's emphases. In this way, managers can conduct a preliminary self-assessment to determine their informational needs, and begin to think about and discuss the subject with their colleagues and subordinates. Naturally, the same instrument could be re-administered in the weeks following the training to determine the training's impact on the acquisition and retention of information.

In the United States, the Conference Board conducted a survey in 1992 designed to document employers' experiences with work–family education and training programmes for managers. In addition, numerous interviews were conducted with expert trainers and corporate representatives. The results of this survey underscore several critical themes related to both the content and format of such training:

- The most important information for middle managers includes knowledge about how work–family programmes affect the bottom-line, techniques and skills for managing flexible work arrangements, knowledge of the company's existing work–family programmes and policies, and recognition of managers' own attitudes toward work-family issues.
- For senior managers, it is more important to educate them about the competitive advantages of work–family initiatives, as well as how such initiatives relate to other company policies and programmes, than to focus on issues of implementation.
- It is essential to provide managers at all levels with information about what their competitors are doing in the area. 'Benchmarking' introduces a measure of external pressure as a prod to change.
- As Figure 5.2 reveals, an abundance of methods and media have been used to educate managers (and in some instances employees as well) regarding the subject, the single measure rated most effective being a public statement by the CEO not only endorsing managerial flexibility but lauding and championing it. In one organization, the CEO attended a work–family forum composed of more than 150 middle managers, and announced that, in his view, employees' families were their first priority.

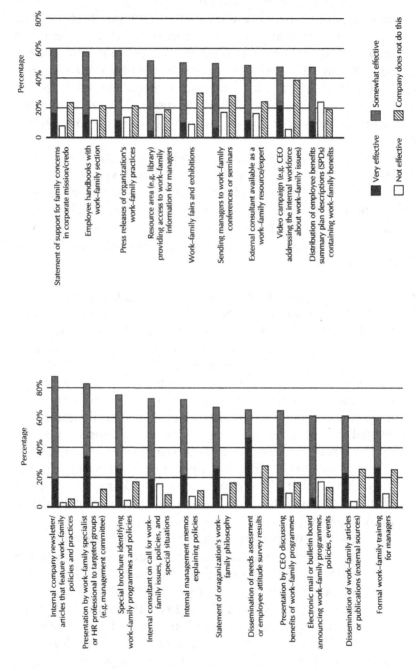

Figure 5.2 Various education methods and how they are working. Reproduced by permission of the Conference Board

- Because people learn by example, training programmes should build in many real-life scenarios, case studies, and success stories. In this way, enlightened managers who have creatively handled tough requests for flexible work arrangements can share their experiences with managers who are more sceptical or closed-minded, or who simply need guidance about ways of meeting both personal and organizational needs fairly and consistently.
- Flexibility training should not be handled as a stand-alone enterprise; it must be linked to other central organizational values and to the corporate credo. For example, it must be congruent with employment equity, diversity, employee development, and human rights policies and practices.
- Although managers need policy statements, procedures, and guidelines to create legitimacy and structure around the flexibility, training must not appear to restrict managers' discretion in adjudicating requests for and implementing alternative work arrangements. Above all, managers must retain the autonomy to deny or defer requests, and to negotiate customized arrangements. In fact, one of the primary training goals should be to effect a sea change in managers' stance— from treating everyone the same to treating everyone fairly on the basis of their needs and circumstances. Furthermore, managers should not leave training with the belief that they must grant every request they receive or suffer the accusation of being biased. Instead, they should come away believing that they have the knowledge and skills to determine whether or not a request can be accommodated in the light of existing policies and business needs.

Other useful suggestions for training on this subject include the use of charts displaying the demographic characteristics of the organization's workforce in order to drive home the message of diversity in lifestyles, family contexts, and caregiving responsibilities. Similarly, sessions can include information about the costs of training new employees because one of the principal rationales for flexibility is that it helps employers to retain and attract high quality employees. Training sessions could also be kicked off with a short quiz (see Box 5.1) that sensitizes managers to the varied ways that work and family intersect, and the dilemmas that arise

---

Box 5.1   *A Work and Family Quiz*

The following questions don't necessarily have right or wrong answers. For everybody who says the answer is obvious, there is probably somebody on the other side who feels the answer is equally obvious. But one thing is certain: as the line between work and family blurs, hard questions such as these will have to be addressed, and consensus won't be easy.

1.

Is it okay for someone to bring their baby to work on an emergency basis?
   Would the sex of the parent make a difference in your answer?
   Would the sex of the parent make a difference in your perception of the worker?
   Does it make a difference whether the worker is a professional or a clerical worker? If the worker has a private office?

2.

An employee works from home part of the time, putting in the same hours as his colleagues at the office. But whenever the boss calls, the boss can hear the sound of children in the background. The boss knows that any business callers will hear the same noises. Is that a problem?
   Are the sounds of children playing more disturbing than the typical sounds of an office?

3.

Should a boss praise an employee for flying to Japan on business the day after his wife gave birth? Similarly, should a boss praise a worker in a memo to the entire staff, noting that the worker was so committed to the success of a major project that her infant son didn't recognize her when she came home from a three-week business trip?

4.

A divorced father, who doesn't get to see his eight-year-old daughter often, wants to bring her into the office after her early school dismissal every Wednesday at 2 p.m., as well as on her vacations. She is perfectly well-behaved, reading quietly by his desk. Should she be allowed to come to the office?
   What if other workers complain that they feel inhibited using even mildly foul language when the child is around?
   What if the boss feels inhibited in even mildly correcting the worker in front of his daughter?
   What if three other parents want to bring their equally well-behaved children in once a week?

5.

Should a boss ask subordinates if they want to buy her daughter's Girl Scout cookies?
   What if the person isn't selling to the subordinates, but colleagues?

6.

Should a woman promise to return from maternity leave, even though she isn't sure she will?

(continued)

What if she is pretty sure she won't return, but wants to leave open the possibility of keeping her old job? She knows that if she says she probably won't return, her old job will be filled.

7.

Is it okay for a worker to interrupt a conversation with a subordinate or peer to take a call from her spouse? How about from her children? How about from her best friend?

8.

Is it okay for a boss to schedule regular Friday staff meetings at 7:30 a.m.?
How about if it's an informal, but mandatory, meeting on Saturday at the boss's house? Does it make a difference if spouses and children are invited?

9.

If a woman says she is late for work because of parental responsibilities, is it perceived differently than when it's a man? Assume it happens, at most, once a month.
If it happens more frequently, are men and women perceived differently?

10.

Is it okay for a worker to make a five-minute phone call to his children every day after school, finding out how their day went and what homework they have? Assume everybody in the office can hear the call.
Does it change your opinion if he's checking in with his mother, to make sure she's okay?
How about if he spends the same amount of time with a friend, making plans for that evening?

11.

Is it okay for a worker to cover his work area with pictures of his newborn, or drawings scrawled by his young children?
What if all the cubicles in the office are visible to the many business clients who come into the office for meetings?
Should there be a separate rule for workers who have private offices than for those who work in more public areas?

12.

The law notwithstanding, if a manager knows a woman is pregnant, should he consider that when deciding whether to give her a new assignment or asking her to take on something that involves particularly long hours?
Would your answer be the same if the worker is a man whose wife is pregnant or hopes to be?

13.

A worker is asked to spend several months away from home, solving a problem at a factory. He can fly home on the weekends at the company's expense. Should the company pay for accommodations big enough for his wife and two young children to accompany him? Should he ask?

14.

A company is in the midst of a budget squeeze. Salaries are frozen, expenses are trimmed. Is it okay for the company to restrict plum overseas assignments—about the only reward employees can get in tight times—to single workers or childless couples?

(continued)

15.

A manager has an assignment to give out that requests a lot of travel. In deciding whom to give it to, should she consider which workers have small children? Assume that giving the assignment to somebody is tantamount to ordering that person to do it.

16.

Can parents take off one hour each week to go to their child's ball games? Assume they can't make up the time

How about if it's two games a week? Three?

What if a childless worker wants to take off an hour every week to play tennis or go to the movies? Should the parents benefit because of lifestyle choices they make?

17.

A $7\frac{1}{2}$-month pregnant worker is completing an important assignment. The culmination of the project—a formal contract signing—requires a three-hour plane trip. Her doctor would prefer that she does not go, but says it's up to her. The woman wants to see the assignment to its completion. The manager could easily send someone else, but knows that project means a lot to the pregnant woman. What should he do?

18.

If a company hires a husband and wife, should every consideration it makes about one spouse also take into account the other? Does hiring both people, for instance, obligate it to transfer both when it wants to transfer one? Does changing the shift of one require the company to change the shift of the other? Or should it simply treat them as individuals and let them work out potential conflicts?

Would the answers be different if the couple got married after the spouses were working in the company, rather than if they were married when they started working?

19.

Should men start opening doors for a co-worker as soon as they learn she is pregnant?

Should they treat her differently at all?

What should she say if, when she is six months pregnant, her boss comes up to her, pats her stomach, and asks: 'How are my two workers today?'

20.

If clients complain about a job-sharing arrangement because they want full-time service by one representative, should the company eliminate the job sharing? Assume that the company believes that there is no reduction in service as a result of the job sharing.

What if eliminating the job sharing means losing one or both employees?

at this nexus. The quiz could also be published in the company *newsletter as a way of raising consciousness, with prizes* awarded for the most creative or humorous responses.

As Figure 5.2 shows, many companies have featured the work–family theme in their internal newsletters and through electronic mail and bulletin boards. The idea is to communicate and reinforce the message of flexibility through multiple media, featuring success stories and testimony from managers, co-workers, and users of flexible work arrangements. Annual reports, company histories, and press releases are additional vehicles for disseminating word of a change in values and 'pushing the culture' toward greater flexibility. The varied methods companies have used in their work–family training programmes are displayed in Figure 5.3.

USING FLEXIBLE WORK ARRANGEMENTS: SAGE ADVICE FROM THE EXPERIENCED

Interviews, focus groups, and surveys we have conducted in several organizations have been distilled to three sets of insightful suggestions and comments about ways of optimizing the benefits of flexible work arrangements. The first set comes from employees who are using such arrangements, the second from their co-workers, and the third from managers.

ADVICE FROM USERS

Employees who have experience with flexible work arrangements have offered two sets of advice, one set addressing ways of successfully negotiating and performing in such arrangements, and the other set addressing ways of making flexibility a cultural norm within their workplaces.

From the users' perspectives, in order to optimize the success of flexible work arrangements, it is important to:

- Show determination and take a positive approach in the initial planning and negotiation stage with the supervisor or manager.

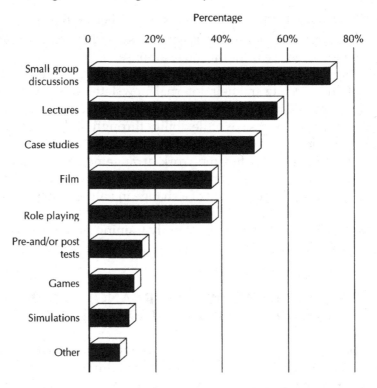

N = 70

Figure 5.3 *In work–family training programme, what methods are used?*
Reproduced by permission of the Conference Board

Experienced users suggest that, when initially approaching one's manager about an alternative work arrangement, it is important to anticipate the barriers that managers and co-workers may place in the way, and then come to the discussion prepared to address ways of overcoming the barriers. Before submitting a proposal to one's manager, discuss the arrangement with co-workers to identify any concerns they may have and to determine ways of modifying the proposed arrangement to prevent problems. In the opinion of Diane Burrus, director of education and training for a consulting firm that specializes in work/family issues: 'The proposal should demonstrate the employee's commitment to the company over the long haul, and an understanding of its corporate goals.'

Users also need to demonstrate their commitment to making

the arrangement work. They need to take a proactive approach to reaching their goal. Users also need to show that they know their job well and have mastered its demands before applying for an alternative arrangement.

- Sensitively and reliably coordinate and communicate with managers and co-workers.

This is a point that all users agreed on, namely that they must consistently inform their co-workers of their schedule in order to prevent misunderstandings that harm productivity and damage personal relationships. As one flexitime user observed:

> My only obstacle in working flex hours is that sometimes other staff members don't understand the agreement. They sometimes expect me to be at the branch when I may have already worked extra hours. The manager does back me up when these situations occur.

Moreover, in return for the extra flexibility they gain through their alternative work arrangement, users must be prepared to temporarily modify their schedule on short notice in order to attend an important department meeting or training session, to accommodate an increase in workload, or to fill in for an absent employee. As one co-worker of a part-time employee noted:

> There is resentment when the part-timers get out of doing overtime during peak periods. However, some employees who have flexible arrangements are excellent about making special efforts to help out.

In short, there are times when users need to show their willingness to place their work ahead of all other commitments, and go the extra distance for their employer in return for the enhanced flexibility they have been granted.

Similarly, users need to build a reliable support system at work so that they have the backup they need and to ensure that they remain 'in the loop'. This entails keeping co-workers advised of one's schedule in advance of any changes, ensuring accessibility through voice mail or computer linkage, and developing at least one close alliance with a co-worker who can handle problems in your absence.

- Show commitment to getting your work done effectively.

Users underscore the importance of demonstrating to others that their first priority is to get their job done well. This entails meeting deadlines, accepting responsibility for oversights and errors, showing willingness to invest extra time when need be, and temporarily suspending the alternative arrangement in order to accommodate exceptional demands at work.

- Discuss your rights and opportunities for advancement.

Although employees who elect a reduced hours arrangement *must be prepared to accept a cut in pay and benefits, they should* discuss how the arrangement may affect their career development. For example, if their schedule precludes attendance at training sessions or at meetings where special assignments are distributed, then their opportunities for advancement may be more limited. Users should also discuss their right to modify their work arrangement and to return to a conventional schedule.

- Discuss the arrangement with family members and gain their support.

Since flexible work arrangements involving a change in the hours or place of work can have pronounced effects on family schedules and on the division of caregiving responsibilities, it is essential to thoroughly review their implications for family life. Ideally, the final arrangement should be determined in concert with those family members who will have to make the greatest adjustments. New schedules are bound to exert radiating effects on domestic tasks, childcare, and leisure time with family members, whereas work-at-home arrangements can affect children's play at home and the boundaries between work and both family time and the use of space.

MAKING FLEXIBILITY A CULTURAL NORM

Users offered the following advice regarding ways of making the organizational culture conducive to flexibility:

- Employers should establish policies and procedures governing flexible work arrangements throughout the organization.

While acknowledging that their managers should have the discretion to grant or refuse a proposal for a flexible work arrangement, employees believe that written policy statements safeguard against managers flatly ruling out such options on the basis of their personal attitudes and stereotypes, their leadership styles, or their perception of risk inherent in such arrangements. Policies would afford greater consistency across the organization, and prevent people from viewing such arrangements as favours and their users as deviants, marginal employees, or specially privileged.

- Employers should offer managers training and rewards for flexibility.

Users believe that managers' attitudes are the greatest impediments to the introduction of flexible work arrangements. Even when policies favouring such arrangements exist, unsupportive managers can sabotage the arrangements, and penalize their users. As one employee observed:

> The manager must truly support the flexible arrangement rather than just going along with it because of company policies when she/he will undermine it because he/she doesn't believe in it. Managers have to care about employees' home/personal lives.

Hence, managers need to understand how such arrangements can be strategically employed to retain valuable personnel, maintain or increase productivity, and improve morale and loyalty. Furthermore, users feel that attitude change can be best effected through the testimony of their peers who have successfully implemented such arrangements, as well as by making flexibility a criterion in managers' performance evaluations. Users also feel that managers can take more initiative in proposing flexible work arrangements for employees who they feel could handle and benefit from them. When managers learn that some problems can be solved by implementing flexible work arrangements, it nudges the culture toward greater flexibility.

- Employers should make alternative career paths available to the users of flexible work arrangements.

Much of the hesitation about requesting and entering flexible work arrangements stems from worries about their implications for job security and advancement. This is clearly illustrated in the following remarks of a bank employee who had been working on a reduced hours schedule for many years:

> I have been on three or four days a week since 1986, and although I am
> consistently a top achiever, and rated on team reports as 'four' (highly
> competent), there has been no grade level advancement accorded me,
> and there seems to be no possibility to advance to another, higher level
> position as there are none available either as job sharing or 30 hours a
> week. So the work and lifestyle programme (the bank's flexibility initiat-
> ive) is more viewed as the bank helping out an employee for a short-term
> time period until they're ready to get back to work full-time.

This quotation aptly describes employers' biased perceptions of part-time employees as marginal and dispensable, and as having little organizational commitment or interest in career development. They have also been seen as employees who lack the dedication, energy, or skill to cope with both family and job demands. Hence, it is essential to legitimize alternative arrangements by offering the users opportunities for career development and advancement.

- Employers need to 'walk the talk'; flexibility must be shown at the highest management levels.

Users suggest that cultural change will not occur until senior management models and rewards flexibility. At present, too many of those in the senior ranks have advanced because of their willingness to invest long hours at work, and continue to do so in their present positions. As the following remarks of a bank manager reveal, managers themselves recognize that they are behaving in ways that are inconsistent with policies favouring flexibility:

> At the management level, our delivery on concerns raised through the
> work and lifestyle programme (the bank's flexibility initiative) has not
> been great. I believe myself, my boss, and our supervisor are poor role
> models as my normal work week is 55–60 hours, and those who report to
> me directly sometimes feel uncomfortable about 'leaving early' even
> though they are putting in a 42–50 hour week. We need to do a better job
> of leading by example, as we do set the tone.

Users argue that the best way to persuade employees that a flexible arrangement is not a poison pill for their career, a ghetto for the fragile, or a stepping stone to unemployment, is to spotlight senior managers who are successfully using alternative arrangements. The impact of only one senior executive who 'walks the talk' is far greater than the numerous pronouncements and exhortations for flexibility from the upper echelons.

ADVICE FROM CO-WORKERS

Colleagues who work alongside the users of flexible arrangements are in critical positions to either make the arrangement
work or to subvert it. They can be allies or adversaries, depending on their perceptions of the arrangement's impact on their
personal functioning and prospects for advancement at work,
and on their unit's performance and morale. For these reasons, it
is critical to take into regard co-workers' initial opinions and
suggestions about how to set up the arrangement, and then to
stay in touch with them to monitor the arrangement's ongoing
impacts and do any troubleshooting that is called for.

From the perspectives of co-workers, in order to optimize the
success of flexible work arrangements, it is important to:

- Ensure that flexible arrangements do not unfairly burden
  co-workers, restrict their flexibility, or leave them with the
  'dirty work'.

This advice is aptly reflected in the following two quotations
from co-workers of persons using flexible arrangements. The
first quotation illustrates the sense of unfairness that can arise
when co-workers lose options that were once available to them:
*'Because the people using flexible arrangements always want Fridays
off, it is hard for regular employees to ever get a Friday off'*. The second
quotation illuminates the sense of injustice that arises among
co-workers when they perceive that tasks are unfairly distributed because of the need to accommodate part-time employees:

> In some areas, part-time workers get all the interesting project work and
> no day to day 'administrivia'. In other areas, it is the reverse. These
> discrepancies always lead to a sense of unfairness.

It follows that co-workers advise users to take the entire unit's
needs into account when they first propose a flexible arrangement, and to recognize that the users must show flexibility in
order for co-workers to show flexibility toward them. For
example, it may be necessary for users to come to key meetings at
off-work times, and to work extra hours on time-sensitive tasks.
Users should also periodically solicit their colleagues' input
about how the arrangement is working out. If the feedback is not
entirely positive, then users should try to address these concerns.

Co-workers agree that if users make an effort to fine-tune the arrangement, their colleagues will usually try to meet them half way.

• Constantly communicate and coordinate with co-workers.

This admonition is echoed by virtually every co-worker. It refers to the importance of users keeping their colleagues well informed in advance about changes in their schedules and locations, the best ways and times to make personal contact, and about any assistance they will require to get their work done. On the latter score, co-workers feel that they are often called upon to substitute and provide back-up for people using flexible arrangements, such as fielding urgent questions or meeting with a client when the user is unavailable. Moreover, co-workers expect and appreciate reciprocity from users, which is best demonstrated by their willingness to temporarily alter their schedules or to pick up the slack for a co-worker. As one co-worker observed:

> A team approach is very important. People can't define their own jobs too narrowly or individualistically. Everyone has to have a sense of responsibility towards helping each other, and covering for each other. You aren't doing the other person a favour because you're all part of a team.

• Be supportive, understanding, and realistic in your stance toward users.

Although co-workers agree that users do not need to disclose why they have opted for a flexible arrangement, they feel that trust, patience, support, and empathy are essential ingredients of effective relationships with users. They also feel it is important to be realistic about the quantity of work that can be accomplished by a colleague who has been granted a reduced hours arrangement, a theme that underlies the larger challenge of developing a shared understanding of mutual expectations.

ADVICE FROM MANAGERS

Naturally, managers have abundant advice about how to improve attitudes and overcome resistance to flexible arrangements, how to negotiate and implement them with employees, and how to evaluate the impacts on their own and their unit's functioning, as well as on the culture and practices of the organization.

From managers' perspectives, in order to optimize the success of flexible work arrangements, it is important to:

- Collaboratively design, implement, and monitor flexible arrangements.

Although managers agree that the initiative should come from employees themselves, they believe that the details of the arrangement, as well as any new accountability mechanisms it requires, should be mutually established. Many managers suggest a six month review in order to air problems, assess progress, make adjustments, and plan for the future. Such reviews could prevent individuals from becoming cynical toward the employer's commitment to flexibility, a sentiment that is expressed in the following quotation from a flexitime initiate:

> Flexitime is given lip-service; as soon as we try it we are told it is not working. Not enough time or adequate review is given to see if it is indeed working.

It is also advisable to agree with the employee in advance about the means of assessing performance under the new arrangement. For example, coordination and communication may be given higher priority in future performance evaluations and, consequently, the parties will need to agree about the co-workers who will be consulted regarding these two domains. More generally, managers believe that it is essential to clearly define the terms of the arrangement, including all details of the hours, compensation, benefits, equipment and space usage, and provisions for modification and termination of the arrangement.

- Retain the prerogative to refuse or terminate a flexible arrangement if it is bad for business.

Managers with experience underscore the importance of retaining the discretion to turn down, adjust, or terminate a flexible arrangement that they judge not to be in the organization's best interests. Although they welcome policies, procedure manuals, and guidelines which bestow legitimacy on the arrangements and ensure a measure of consistency across the organization, managers feel that they must weigh the potential or actual costs and benefits of the arrangement for their own unit, and that only they can determine whether an employee is personally and vocationally well suited to a proposed or actual arrangement. Moreover, while emphasizing that managers should be open to any and all requests, managers should also be prepared to suggest alternative arrangements and suggest trial arrangements when they harbour doubts about any proposal. Managers may also wish to issue memos regarding the application of company policies to their own unit, identifying the types of positions and arrangements that they deem possible and those that are not suited to the unit's activities. In this regard, one manager observed:

> I have more functional jobs within my area where I'm much more reluctant to go with flexible arrangements because of the job requirements. However, I will assess all requests and determine if the person should be moved to another position (in the company) to accommodate their needs.

- Look for opportunities to use flexible arrangements as a strategic management tool.

As managers gain comfort deploying their workforce in more flexible ways, they will need to develop creative solutions to workforce problems. For example, when a large bank lost several tellers due to maternity leaves, the manager drew on a list of former tellers who had quit to have babies and found many of them delighted to return on a part-time basis as a respite from the demands of childcare. Similarly, many companies maintain a list of temporary workers, including retirees, who are prepared to fill in for permanent workers who are on vacation or to supplement the workforce during periods of peak demand. Employers have also rotated workers through a number of different jobs and then availed themselves of such cross-training when they need to fill in for or replace someone.

- Beware of misconceptions and blinkered views of flexible arrangements and their users.

Managers need to consider and discuss their assumptions about how, when, and where work is best accomplished. Through dialogue, they will learn to debunk the myths that 'one size fits all', productivity hinges on close supervision, and that the best employees are those who leave their personal and family concerns at the workplace door. Similarly, managers need to reexamine their stance toward those who apply for and use flexible arrangements. In the words of a senior advisor and champion of work/family initiatives at a Canadian bank:

> If someone is working part-time, does that mean they are less committed to their career than someone working full-time? The preconception is 'Yes', but it's not true. If they were good as a full-time employee, they will be equally good part-time.

• Link workplace flexibility to other key business themes, such as diversity, equity, leadership, and quality assurance.

Through discussion, managers will come to view flexible work arrangements as ways of recognizing the needs of a diverse workforce that includes people with different religious customs, ethnic backgrounds, and cultural heritages. They will learn that flexibility offers a means of accommodating expressions of diversity in the workplace that take the forms of requests for leaves, a change in hours, or a work-at-home arrangement. Moreover, the granting of flexible arrangements can give rise to equity concerns on the part of managers who wish to avoid the appearance of giving preference to one request or employee over another. Experienced managers understand that they are being asked to address individual needs in a consistently fair manner, not that they are extending special favours to individuals or that they should be doing the same thing for everyone.

SUMMARY

As work organizations shift toward using a broader range of scheduling options and deploying personnel in more varied locations, managers will need to take a more fluid approach to the supervision of employees, and commit themselves to helping employees achieve a healthy balance between their job and their personal responsibilities. Organizations that have been most successful in designing a flexible workplace have squarely faced the varied sources of resistance and scepticism that first greet messages about such policy changes. Mainly, they have overcome the objections and recalcitrance by directly addressing these concerns, and then persuading managers of the viability of flexible arrangements by sharing success stories told by peers who have successfully managed the process of change. In addition, successful implementation of these arrangements has depended on a planned and gradual transformative process, one which allows much room for testing, fine-tuning, and reformulating policy and practice.

By creating the conditions that give workers a greater sense of control over their time and their jobs, and by promoting a greater measure of harmony between their lives at work and at home, employers are likely to master the challenge of meeting the competitive needs of industry as well as the personal needs of employees.

6

Toolkit: Assessing Needs and Effects

This chapter presents a set of tools that can be used to assess the need for, and effects of, flexible work arrangements. The self-scoring tools are based on the CARNET *Work and Home Life Survey* described in Chapter Four. They provide a 'snapshot' of the employee's candidacy for and functioning in a flexible work arrangement.

In adopting a self-scoring format, we aimed to provide a set of tools that could be applied by two groups of readers. First, employees can use the tools to perform their own assessment of whether and how they would benefit from a flexible work arrangement. Employees currently using a flexible work arrangement can also use the tools to gauge the effectiveness of their arrangement in meeting their personal needs. In sum, the tools and comparative data we provide will allow employees to make an assessment of whether: (a) they should consider switching to a flexible work arrangement; or (b) if they are already in such an arrangement, whether their current arrangement is effective in allowing them to balance competing demands.

Second, managers can use the tools to assist employees to determine: (a) whether or not they may need a flexible work arrangement; or (b) whether their current arrangement is meeting their needs. By having an employee complete the tools and then referring to the interpretative data we provide, managers will have a more objective and comprehensive basis for decision-making.

There are three sets of tools. The first set assesses the current work situation. Specifically, the tools assess: (a) perceptions of current work load; (b) perceptions of the amount of control over time at work; (c) job satisfaction; and (d) the amount of full and partial absenteeism the employee is currently experiencing at work.

The second set of tools assesses family household and dependent responsibilities, including: (a) responsibilities for household chores; (b) responsibilities for childcare; and (c) responsibilities for eldercare. Although this is not an exhaustive list of family responsibilities, the tools assess the major types of family responsibilities assumed by employees.

The third set of tools assesses four dimensions of work and family conflict including: (a) the extent to which work interferes with family (both time-based and strain-based conflict); and (b) the extent to which family demands interfere with work (both time-based and strain-based conflict). In addition, the final tool in this section assesses the employee's current experience of stress.

USING THE TOOLS

Scores can be computed after each tool is completed, or the individual can complete all the tools and then score them. For each scale, scoring consists of two simple steps.

Step 1: For each vertical column add up the numbers you have circled and place the total in the space provided at the bottom of the column.

Step 2: Add the column totals together to get your *total score* for that scale.

INTERPRETING THE SCORES

After each scale is scored, the individual can look up the interpretation of the score in the following section. The score interpretations or norms are based on responses from over 1700 employees who completed the *Work and Home Life Survey*.

SET I: CURRENT WORK SITUATION

Work Overload

How much do you agree or disagree with each of the following statements about your job?

1 Strongly Disagree	2 Disagree	3 Neutral	4 Agree	5 Strongly Agree

For each item, circle the number corresponding to your answer.

1.	I have enough time to complete my work.	5	4	3	2	1
2.	In my job, I have too much to do.	1	2	3	4	5
3.	I can rarely finish the work I have to do.	1	2	3	4	5
4.	I usually have time on my hands.	5	4	3	2	1

+ ___ + ___ + ___ + ___

TOTAL SCORE _____

Control at Work

How much do you agree or disagree with each of the following statements about your job?

1 Strongly Disagree	2 Disagree	3 Neutral	4 Agree	5 Strongly Agree

For each item, circle the number corresponding to your answer.

1.	I decide how to spend my time at work.	1	2	3	4	5
2.	I have little say over when I start and stop work.	5	4	3	2	1
3.	I have control over how fast I have to work.	1	2	3	4	5
4.	Other people at work decide how my work gets done.	5	4	3	2	1
5.	I have a rigid schedule.	5	4	3	2	1
6.	I have a say in deciding my work schedule.	1	2	3	4	5

+ ___ + ___ + ___ + ___

TOTAL SCORE _____

Job Satisfaction

Using the scale below, please circle the number that best describes how satisfied or dissatisfied you are with each of the following.

1 Very Dissatified	2 Dissatisfied	3 Neutral	4 Satisfied	5 Very Satisfied

1.	The salary you receive.	1	2	3	4	5
2.	The benefits you receive.	1	2	3	4	5
3.	Your total compensation package.	1	2	3	4	5
4.	The amount of supervision you receive.	1	2	3	4	5
5.	The quality of supervision you receive.	1	2	3	4	5
6.	The way your supervisor treats you.	1	2	3	4	5
7.	The cooperation you get from co-workers.	1	2	3	4	5
8.	The way you and your co-workers get along personally.	1	2	3	4	5
9.	The support you get from co-workers.	1	2	3	4	5
10.	The amount of work you have to do.	1	2	3	4	5
11.	The type of work you have to do.	1	2	3	4	5
12.	The chance you have to use your skills.	1	2	3	4	5
13.	The chance you have to get ahead.	1	2	3	4	5
14.	Your job security.	1	2	3	4	5
15.	The fairness of promotion policies.	1	2	3	4	5

+   +   +   +

TOTAL SCORE _____

Absenteeism

Partial Absence

In the **past six months** did any of the following happen?

1 Never/not Applicable
2 Once a month or less
3 Two or three times per month
4 Once a week
5 Several times a week
6 Every day

For each item, circle the number
corresponding to your answer.

1.	I was unable to concentrate at work.	1	2	3	4	5	6
2.	I had to interrupt my workday to deal with non-work matters.	1	2	3	4	5	6
3.	I had to leave work early.	1	2	3	4	5	6
4.	I had to take an extended lunch hour.	1	2	3	4	5	6
5.	I had to come in late.	1	2	3	4	5	6

       +   +   +   +   +

TOTAL SCORE _____

Full-day Absence

There are times when things happen and we have to be absent from work. Please think about the amount of time you have had to take off from work in the **past six months**. **DO NOT** include vacation days, statutory holidays or your normal days off.

In the past six months, how many days in total were you absent from work? (Please circle the appropriate number)

0 1 2 3 4 5 6 7 8 9 10 11 12 13 14 15 16 17 18 19 20+

SET II: FAMILY RESPONSIBILITIES

These are activities you do for yourself and for any other people **who live in the same household as you.** Please indicate how often you do each activity.

1 *Never/Not Applicable*
2 *Once a month or less*
3 *Two or three times per month*
4 *Once a week*
5 *Several times a week*
6 *Every day*
For each item, circle the number
corresponding to your answer.

1.	Meal preparation and clean-up	1	2	3	4	5	6
2.	House cleaning	1	2	3	4	5	6
3.	Laundry	1	2	3	4	5	6

4.	Property and/or garden maintenance	1	2	3	4	5	6
5.	Financial affairs/planning	1	2	3	4	5	6
6.	Grocery shopping	1	2	3	4	5	6
7.	Other shopping (e.g. clothes)	1	2	3	4	5	6

      +   +   +   +   +

TOTAL SCORE _____

Childcare

Family caregiving involves help you may be providing to immediate family members and relatives. First, we ask about your childcare responsibilities. If you do not provide childcare please feel free to skip this tool.

> 1 *Never/Not Applicable*
> 2 *Once a month or less*
> 3 *Two or three times per month*
> 4 *Once a week*
> 5 *Several times a week*
> 6 *Every day*
> For each item, circle the number corresponding to your answer.

Do you help them with these basic things?

1.	Eating	1	2	3	4	5	6
2.	Bathing	1	2	3	4	5	6
3.	Dressing	1	2	3	4	5	6
4.	Toileting/changing nappies	1	2	3	4	5	6
5.	Taking medication	1	2	3	4	5	6

Do you help them with these practical things?

1.	Transporting them to places or events.	1	2	3	4	5	6
2.	Attending appointments with or about them.	1	2	3	4	5	6
3.	Watching/supervising them.	1	2	3	4	5	6
4.	Laundry.	1	2	3	4	5	6
5.	Shopping needs.	1	2	3	4	5	6
6.	Household chores.	1	2	3	4	5	6
7.	Home maintenance/garden work.	1	2	3	4	5	6
8.	Meal preparation	1	2	3	4	5	6
9.	Getting around inside or outside the home.	1	2	3	4	5	6

Do you help them with any of these personal services?

1.	Arranging for their care while you are absent.	1	2	3	4	5	6
2.	Arranging other medical/social services for them.	1	2	3	4	5	6
3.	Giving them money.	1	2	3	4	5	6
4.	Money management.	1	2	3	4	5	6
5.	Completing forms and other paperwork.	1	2	3	4	5	6
6.	Planning activities for them.	1	2	3	4	5	6

And, finally, do you help any of them in these other ways?

1.	When a sudden illness, injury or crisis occurs.	1	2	3	4	5	6
2.	When someone else can't take care of them.	1	2	3	4	5	6
3.	With their emotional difficulties.	1	2	3	4	5	6
4.	With their mood swings or extreme behaviours.	1	2	3	4	5	6

+   +   +   +   +

TOTAL SCORE _____

Eldercare

Eldercare involves help you may be providing to elderly family members and relatives. If you do not provide eldercare, please feel free to skip this tool.

> 1 *Never/Not Applicable*
> 2 *Once a month or less*
> 3 *Two or three times per month*
> 4 *Once a week*
> 5 *Several times a week*
> 6 *Every day*
> For each item, circle the number corresponding to your answer.

Do you help them with these basic things?

1.	Eating	1	2	3	4	5	6
2.	Bathing	1	2	3	4	5	6
3.	Dressing	1	2	3	4	5	6
4.	Toileting/changing an absorbent undergarment	1	2	3	4	5	6
5.	Taking medication	1	2	3	4	5	6

Do you help them with these practical things?

1.	Transporting them to places or events.	1	2	3	4	5	6
2.	Attending appointments with or about them.	1	2	3	4	5	6
3.	Watching/supervising them.	1	2	3	4	5	6
4.	Helping with laundry.	1	2	3	4	5	6
5.	Shopping needs.	1	2	3	4	5	6
6.	Household chores.	1	2	3	4	5	6
7.	Home maintenance/garden work.	1	2	3	4	5	6
8.	Meal preparation	1	2	3	4	5	6
9.	Getting around inside or outside the home.	1	2	3	4	5	6

Do you help them with any of these personal services?

1.	Arranging for their care while you are absent.	1	2	3	4	5	6
2.	Arranging other medical/social services for them.	1	2	3	4	5	6
3.	Giving them money.	1	2	3	4	5	6
4.	Money management.	1	2	3	4	5	6
5.	Completing forms and other paperwork.	1	2	3	4	5	6
6.	Planning activities for them.	1	2	3	4	5	6

And, finally, do you help any of them in these other ways?

1.	When a sudden illness, injury or crisis occurs.	1	2	3	4	5	6
2.	When someone else can't take care of them.	1	2	3	4	5	6
3.	With their emotional difficulties.	1	2	3	4	5	6
4.	With their mood swings or extreme behaviors.	1	2	3	4	5	6
5.	With their mental disabilities such as serious memory problems.	1	2	3	4	5	6
6.	With their confusion about things.	1	2	3	4	5	6

___ + ___ + ___ + ___ + ___

TOTAL SCORE _____

SET III: WORK AND FAMILY CONFLICT

Work Interference With Family

Using the scale shown below, please indicate how often the following things happen to you.

1	2	3	4
Never	Sometimes	Often	Almost Always

For each item, circle the number that corresponds to your answer.

Time Based

1.	I have to change plans with family members because of the demands of my job.	1	2	3	4
2.	Job demands keep me from spending the amount of time I would like with my family.	1	2	3	4
3.	Job responsibilities make it difficult for me to get family chores/errands done.	1	2	3	4
4.	To meet the demands of my job, I have to limit the number of things I do with family members.	1	2	3	4
5.	My job prevents me from attending appointments and special events for family members.	1	2	3	4

___ + ___ + ___ + ___

TOTAL SCORE _____

Strain Based

1.	After work, I have little energy left for the things I need to do at home.	1	2	3	4
2.	I do not listen to what people at home are saying because I am thinking about work.	1	2	3	4
3.	After work, I just need to be left alone for a while.	1	2	3	4
4.	My job puts me in a bad mood at home.	1	2	3	4
5.	The demands of my job make it hard for me to enjoy the time I spend with my family.	1	2	3	4
6.	I think about work when I am at home.	1	2	3	4

___ + ___ + ___ + ___

TOTAL SCORE _____

Family Interference with Work

Time Based

1.	I would put in a longer work day if I had fewer family demands.	1	2	3	4
2.	My family demands interrupt my work day.	1	2	3	4
3.	Family demands make it difficult for me to take on additional job responsibilities.	1	2	3	4
4.	I spend time at work making arrangements for family members.	1	2	3	4
5.	Family demands make it difficult for me to have the work schedule I want.	1	2	3	4

+ + +

TOTAL SCORE _____

Strain Based

1.	When I am at work, I am distracted by my family demands.	1	2	3	4
2.	Things going on in my family life make it difficult for me to concentrate at work.	1	2	3	4
3.	Events at home make me tense and irritable on the job.	1	2	3	4
4.	Because of the demands I face at home, I am tired at work.	1	2	3	4
5.	I spend time at work thinking about the things that I have to get done at home.	1	2	3	4
6.	My family life puts me in a bad mood at work.	1	2	3	4

+ + +

TOTAL SCORE _____

Stress

Thinking about how you have been feeling in the **past month**, have you:

1 Never	2 Almost Never	3 Some of the Time	4 Most of the Time	5 All of the Time

For each item, circle the number corresponding to your answer.

1.	Felt overwhelmed by things.	1	2	3	4	5
2.	Felt good about life.	1	2	3	4	5
3.	Felt anxious and/or worried.	1	2	3	4	5
4.	Been able to handle stress.	1	2	3	4	5
5.	Felt tired and worn out.	1	2	3	4	5
6.	Felt calm and/or relaxed.	1	2	3	4	5
7.	Had trouble concentrating.	1	2	3	4	5
8.	Felt full of energy.	1	2	3	4	5
9.	Felt unable to cope.	1	2	3	4	5
10.	Felt in control.	1	2	3	4	5

       +   +   +   +

TOTAL SCORE _____

SCORING AND INTERPRETATION GUIDELINES

Set I: Current Work Situation

The tools in this section assess your perceptions of: (a) work overload; (b) control over time; (c) job satisfaction; and (d) absenteeism.

The sense of job overload results from two inter-related factors. First, overload is frequently associated with the sheer number of tasks that have to be completed during the day. Second, overload is frequently associated with a sense of time pressure. Higher scores on the scale indicate more job overload. Our studies have suggested that the sense of job overload is strongly associated with negative outcomes such as stress.

The perception of control over time is also an important predictor of stress. Our scale measures the extent to which you feel you have the freedom to decide when you schedule certain tasks in the day. A low sense of control (indicated by low scores on the scale) is frequently associated with symptoms of stress, while higher scores indicate a more healthy work environment.

The job satisfaction tool assesses the extent to which you are satisfied with various aspects of your job. Higher scores on the tool generally indicate greater satisfaction.

Finally, we provide two measures of absenteeism; partial absenteeism and full-day absence. Partial absenteeism refers to those occasions when you are physically present at work but unable to concentrate on the tasks at hand because you are preoccupied with non-work related matters. Partial absenteeism also includes the occasions when you take less than a full day off work by coming in late, leaving early, or taking an extended lunch hour. In contrast full-day absence refers to those occasions when you have had to miss at least one full day of work.

Work Overload

If you scored:

Less than 8. Scores less than eight indicate a very low level of work overload. You typically have enough time in the day to complete your work and rarely feel pressured.

Between 8 and 15.   Scores in this range suggest a moderate amount of work overload. Occasionally, you feel pressured at work, with too much to do in too little time.

More than 15. Scores above 15 suggest a high level of work overload. Most likely, you frequently feel as though 'there are not enough hours in the day' to complete your tasks. If you score in this range, a flexible work arrangement is worth considering.

Control

If you scored:

Less than 16. If you scored less than 16 on this tool, your score indicates a very low degree of control at work. Essentially, you see your time as almost completely controlled by other people. If you scored within this range, flexible work arrangements (particularly arrangements such as telecommuting or flexible work hours that increase control over time) might be worth considering.

Between 16 and 23. This represents an 'average' score. Like most of us, your time is neither completely under your own control nor completely dictated by others. Again, scores in this range might lead you to consider a flexible work arrangement.

More than 23. You have a great deal of control over your worktime. Because of the high level of control you already have, a flexible work arrangement is unlikely to increase your control over time at work.

Job Satisfaction

If you scored:

Less than 45. Scores less than 45 indicate a low level of satisfaction with your job. If you scored within this range it is worth reviewing your answers to see if you are expressing a low level of satisfaction with most aspects of your job or whether there are specific aspects of your job (i.e. the type of work, the compensation, your co-workers, your supervisor) that you are most dissatisfied with. Depending on how you answered the questions, a flexible work arrangement might be worth considering.

Between 45 and 61. Scores in this range indicate an average level of job satisfaction. Although there may be specific aspects of your job that you dislike, you are generally satisfied with most aspects of your job.

More than 61.   Scores in this range represent a high level of job satisfaction. You are probably at least moderately satisfied with all aspects of your job.

Absenteeism

Partial Absence

If you scored:

Less than 7. Scores in this range indicate a low level of partial absence. While at work you are generally 'on task' and your workday is rarely disrupted by non-work influences.

Between 7 and 11. Scores in this range indicate a moderate level of partial absence. Although you are generally able to attend to your work tasks, there are times when disruptions, non-work influences, or an inability to concentrate detracts from your ability to focus on the job. However, these disruptions do not happen frequently.

More than 11. Scores above 11 suggest a high level of partial absence (maximum score on the scale is 25). Particularly if your scores approach the scale maximum, you may wish to consider whether a flexible work arrangement would allow you to minimize disruptions in your workday.

Full-day Absence

If you scored:

Less than 2. If you indicated missing less than two days work in the last six months, you have indicated a fairly low level of full-day absence.

Between 3 and 5. This is a moderate level of full day absence. You might want to consider the factors that caused you to miss these days at work and whether flexible work arrangements would assist you in balancing competing demands on your time.

More than 5. This is a high level of full day absence. Scores in this range can be discounted if you had experienced a major illness or injury (e.g. car accident) that caused you to miss an extended period at work. However, if most of your absences were short (i.e. one day at a time), then you should consider the demands that are being placed on your time and whether a flexible work arrangement would help you to achieve a better balance.

Set II: Caregiving Responsibilities

In this section, we consider three aspects of your non-work responsibilities. We focus on family caregiving because for most people the family represents the major non-work responsibilities in their lives.

We consider three aspects of family caregiving. The first type of family responsibilities refers to the household chores and maintenance that we all experience, regardless of whether we have children or elderly dependants. There is a significant amount of work involved in simply keeping a household running. Our tool assesses your involvement in such activities.

Second, childcare is perhaps the most common form of family caregiving. Although it may seem obvious that children require care, our tool assesses the extent of *your* involvement in such caregiving. That is, different family members may provide different levels or types of care to children. While many researchers have focussed on indirect or proxy measures of caregiving, such as the number and ages of children in the home, we have found that this is a poor gauge of the amount of time and work that parents actually invest in childcare and supervision. For this reason, we measure the frequency of engaging in different types of caregiving activity.

Finally, like childcare, involvement in eldercare can imply a range of activities, from taking an elderly relative shopping to providing personal nursing care. Again, we have found it most useful to focus on both the frequency and type of activities individuals engage in as part of their eldercare responsibilities.

Family Responsibilities

If you scored:

Less than 16. Scores in this range indicate a low level of family responsibilities. If you scored in this range, you have indicated that you do not have the primary responsibility for most aspects of keeping a household running, although you may assume primary responsibility for some activities (e.g. garden work, property maintenance).

Between 16 and 31. Scores in this range indicate a moderate level of family responsibilities. If you scored in this range, you are doing your share of maintaining a household either by being primarily responsible for some activities or by sharing in most household tasks.

More than 31. If you scored higher than 31, you have indicated a high level of family responsibilities. You are probably assuming primary responsibility for keeping the household running smoothly. It is difficult to reconcile this level of involvement with working full-time hours, and so you might want to consider whether a flexible work arrangement would help you to manage both your work and family responsibilities.

Childcare

If you scored:

Less than 33. Scores in this range indicate a low level of childcare responsibilities. Such scores may result from having older children who are largely self-sufficient. Alternatively, you may have younger children, but you are not assuming the role of primary caregiver for these children.

Between 33 and 93. Scores in this range indicate a moderate level of childcare responsibilities. In terms of your personal involvement in childcare, scores in this range suggest that you assume quite a lot of responsibility; either sharing a broad range of caregiving activities or assuming primary responsibility for certain types of caregiving. Particularly, if you score at the higher end of the range, you may wish to consider using a flexible work arrangement.

More than 93. Scores in this range indicate a very high level of childcare responsibilities. Such scores would be consistent with the role of primary caregiver for small children. If you scored in this range, a flexible work arrangement could be a means for you to reconcile your family and job demands.

Eldercare

If you scored:

Less than 40. Scores in this range indicate a low level of eldercare responsibilities. Such scores may result from having an elderly relative who requires some care, but is largely self-sufficient.

Between 40 and 60. Scores in this range indicate a moderate level of eldercare responsibilities. In terms of your personal involvement in eldercare, scores in this range suggest that you assume quite a lot of responsibility, either sharing a broad range of caregiving activities or assuming primary responsibility for certain types of caregiving. Particularly if these responsibilities are combined with involvement in childcare, you may wish to consider the use of a flexible work arrangement.

More than 60. Scores above 60 represent a high level of eldercare responsibilities that border on providing personal nursing care for an elderly relative. A flexible work arrangement may help you balance these responsibilities with your job and other personal commitments.

Set III: Work and Family Conflict

This set of tools deals with the amount of work and family conflict you experience. Recent research has suggested that work and family conflict can originate in either domain. That is, conflict can arise from work interfering with family life (e.g. working overtime interferes with family activities) or from family demands interfering with work (e.g. illness in the family resulting in absenteeism). Thus, our work and family conflict measures assess both forms of conflict: work interference with family, and family interference with work.

Within each of these types of work and family conflict, there can be one of two forms of conflict, namely time-based and strain-based conflict. Time-based conflict is experienced when time pressures associated with one role prevent the individual from fulfilling the expectations of the other role. For example, the hours and scheduling of work can preempt, disrupt, or limit participation in the family role. Strain-based conflict is experienced when moods, thoughts, and energy depletion associated with one role intrude on and affect performance in the other role.

Work Interference with Family—Time based

If you scored:

Less than 8. A score of less than eight on this scale indicates a low level of time-based work interference with family. In general, your job does not conflict with your homelife either because: (a) your family demands are minimal or easily accommodated outside of work hours; or (b) your current job schedule is flexible enough to allow you to adapt to your family demands without difficulty.

Between 8 and 11. This is a moderate level of time-based work interference with family. A score in this range indicates that you occasionally experience time-based conflicts (for example, having to work overtime or cancel family plans because of work). However, these instances are the exception rather than the rule.

More than 11. A score greater than 11 indicates a high level of time-based work interference with family. If you scored within this range, your responses suggest that you experience conflicts between work and family demands on a fairly regular basis. Especially if you score at the high end of the scale (Note: the maximum score is 20), you will want to investigate strategies to reduce the number of time-based conflicts you experience. Flexible work arrangements are worth considering in this regard.

Work Interference with Family—Strain based

If you scored:

Less than 8. A score less than eight on this scale represents a modest amount of strain-based work interference with family. Your responses suggest that you rarely think about work when you are at home, and that your work generally does not spill over into your personal life.

Between 8 and 14. This is a moderate level of strain-based work interference with family. You occasionally think about work issues while at home or carry the problems of the workday over into your life at home. However, this is not a regular pattern for you or, if it is, it does not cause you much distress at this time.

More than 14. Scores above 14 suggest a high level of strain-based work interference with family. Scores in this range suggest that you frequently think about work while at home, and that this practice is detracting from your ability to fulfil your family responsibilities. For the most part, flexible work arrangements will not address problems caused by strain-based conflict. That is, your score indicates that your job is either very demanding or you are having some acute problems at work. While it is clear that you need to address this issue, flexible work arrangements are not likely to be of much assistance.

Family Interference with Work—Time based

If you scored:

Less than 9. Your score suggests that family demands rarely occur during working hours. As a result you experience very little time-based conflict originating from your family demands.

Between 9 and 14. A score in this range is considered moderate. It suggests that family demands only occasionally intrude on your workday; but this does not happen frequently. Most parents (particularly parents of younger children) score within this range simply due to the occasional medical appointment that has to be scheduled during working hours.

More than 14. Scores above 14 suggest a high level of time-based family interference with work. A score in this range is consistent with a fairly regular intrusion of family demands into the working day. If your score is toward the high end of the scale (maximum score is 20), you may wish to consider a flexible work arrangement. You should think about precisely what type of family interruptions you experience at work and whether or not one of the work arrangements discussed in the book could remedy the problem.

Family Interference with Work—Strain Based

If you scored:

Less than 10. A score of less than 10 indicates a low level of strain-based family interference with work. Scores in this range suggest very infrequent 'spillover' of your family problems into the workplace, suggesting that either: (a) you have very few family demands; or (b) you compartmentalize your family and work responsibilities to a high degree.

Between 10 and 15. Scores in this range indicate a moderate level of strain-based family interference with work. Such scores suggest that family problems or concerns occasionally occupy your thoughts at work, but they are not a constant concern.

More than 15. Scores higher than 15 (maximum score is 24) indicate a high level of strain-based family interference with work. Scores in this range indicate that family concerns frequently occupy your thoughts at work or that your family demands leave you 'drained of energy' by the time you arrive at work. Strain-based family interference with work at this level was only rarely reported by our respondents. High levels are more likely to reflect chronic family problems (e.g. marital discord, unemployment, serious illness) that deplete one's energies. Rather than opting for a work arrangement that offers greater flexibility in the scheduling of hours, you may wish to consider arrangements, such as job sharing and part-time work, that give you more time and energy to focus on your family situation.

Stress

This scale assesses the common symptoms of stress.
If you scored:

Less than 16. Scores in this range indicate that you experience the symptoms of stress infrequently, if at all.

Between 16 and 36. This is the moderate range on the stress scale. Scores in this range suggest that you occasionally experience some of the symptoms of stress, however these experiences are not overwhelming. Most people completing the scale score in this range.

More than 33. Scores in this range (maximum score is 50) indicate a high level of stress. That is, you have indicated that you experience several of the symptoms of stress on a frequent basis. If you scored in this range, you might consider the aspects of your life that are generating the most stress. Depending on your assessment, a flexible work arrangement may help you to cope better with the demands of your life.

CONCLUDING COMMENTS

The scales and interpretations presented in this chapter can be used as tools to assess the need for, and effects of, flexible work arrangements. Naturally, it is impossible to assess every possible circumstance. Nor is it feasible or productive to try to anticipate each individual's circumstances. Individuals are challenged to assess whether their particular *job* and *personal circumstances* and commitments can be more smoothly accommodated through the use of flexible work arrangements. The tools in this chapter, and the guidance contained in preceding chapters, are intended to help individuals appraise their personal 'fit to flex'. Equally important, these tools can assist organizations to become more competitive, adaptive, and resilient in the face of change.

References

Barling, J. & Barenburg, A. (1984). Some personal consequences of "flexitime" work schedules. *Journal of Social Psychology*, **123**, 137–138.

Barling, J. & Gallagher, D.G. (1996). Part-time employment. In C.L. Cooper and I.T. Robertson (Eds.), *International Review of Industrial and Organizational Psychology*, Vol. 11 (pp. 243–278). Chichester, UK: John Wiley and Sons.

Blair, S.L. & Lichter, D.T. (1991). Measuring the division of household labor: Gender segregation of housework among American couples. *Journal of Family Issues*, **12**(1), 91–113.

Buckley, M.R., Kicza, D.C. & Crane, N. (1987). A note on the effectiveness of flextime as an organizational intervention. *Public Personnel Management*, **16**, 259–267.

Calvasina, E.J. & Boxx, W.R. (1975). Efficiency of workers on the four-day work week. *Academy of Management Journal*, **18**, 604–610.

Carnegie Council on Adolescent Development. (1992). *A matter of time: Risk and opportunity in the non-school hours*. New York: Carnegie Corporation.

CARNET: The Canadian Aging Research Network (1993). *The work and family survey findings*. Guelph, Ontario: University of Guelph, Psychology Department.

CARNET: The Canadian Aging Research Network (1994). *The work and homelife survey findings*. Guelph, Ontario: University of Guelph, Psychology Department.

CARNET: The Canadian Aging Research Network (1995). *Flexible work arrangements: A user's guide*. Guelph, Ontario: University of Guelph, Psychology Department.

Coltrin, S.A. & Barendse, B.D. (1981). Is your organization a good candidate for flexitime? *Personnel Journal*, **60**(9), 712–715.

Crouter, A.C. (1984). Spillover from family to work: The neglected side of the work-family interface. *Human Relations*, **37**, 425–441.

Dowler, J.M., Jordan-Simpson, D.A. & Adams, O. (1992). Gender inequalities in caregiving in Canada. *Health Reports*, **4**, 125–136, Statistics Canada cat. 82-003.

Dunham, R.B., Pierce, J.L. & Castaneda, M.B. (1987). Alternative work schedules: Two field quasi-experiments. *Personnel Psychology*, **40**, 215–242.

Duxbury, L., Higgins, C. & Lee, C. (1994). Work-family conflict: A comparison by gender, family type, and perceived control *Journal of Family Issues*, **15**, 449–461.

Dwyer, J. & Seccombe, K. (1991). Elder care as family labor: The influence of gender and family position. *Journal of Family Issues*, **12**, 229–247.

Ferree, M.M. (1991). The gender division of labor in two-earner marriages: Dimensions of variability and change. *Journal of Family Issues*, **12**(2), 158–180.

Friedman, S. (1994). *Linking work-family issues to the bottom line*, Report # 962. Ottawa, Ont: Conference Board of Canada.

Galinsky, E., Bond, J.T. & Friedman, D.E. (1993). *The national study of the changing workforce*. New York: Families and Work Institute.

Galinsky, E. & Stein, P. (1990). The impact of human resource policies on employees: Balancing work/family life. *Journal of Family Issues*, **11**, 368–83.

Golembiewski, R.T. & Proehl, C.W. (1978). A survey of the empirical literature on flexible work hours: Character and consequences of a major innovation. *Academy of Management Review*, **3**, 842–853.

Golembiewski, R.T. & Proehl, C.W. (1980). Public sector applications of flexible workhours: A review of available experience. *Public Administration Review*, **40**, 72–85.

Gutek, B.A., Nakamura, C.Y. & Nieva, V.F. (1981). The interdependence of work and family roles. *Journal of Occupational Behavior*, **2**, 1–16.

Hall, D.T. (1972). A model of coping with role conflict: The role behavior of college educated women. *Administrative Science Quarterly*, **17**, 481-486.

Harrick, E.J., Vanek, G.R. & Michlitsch, J.F. (1986). Alternate work schedules, productivity, leave usage and employee attitudes: A field study. *Public Personnel Management*, **15**, 159–169.

Harris, M.M. & Schaubroeck, J. (1988). A meta-analysis of self-supervisor, self-peer and peer-supervisor ratings. *Personnel Psychology*, **41**, 43–62.

Hartman, R.I. & Weaver, K.M. (1977). Four factors influencing conversion to a four day work week. *Human Resource Management*, 16, 24–27.

Health and Welfare Canada. (1991). *Status of Day Care in Canada*. Ottawa, Ontario: Health and Welfare Canada.

Hewitt Associates. (1995). *Work and family benefits provided by major U.S. employers in 1995*. Lincolnshire, ILL: Hewitt Associates.

Hicks, W.D. & Klimoski, R.J. (1981). The impact of flexitime on employee attitudes. *Academy of Management Journal*, 24, 333–341.

Higgins, C., Duxbury, L. & Lee, C. (1992). *Balancing work and family: A study of Canadian private sector employees*. London, Ontario: National Centre for Management Research and Development.

Hochschild, A. (1989). *The Second Shift*. New York: Viking Press.

Ivancevich, J.M. (1974). Effects of the shorter workweek on selected satisfaction and performance measures. *Journal of Applied Psychology*, 59, 717–721.

Ivancevich, J.M. & Lyon, H.L. (1977). The shortened workweek: A field experiment. *Journal of Applied Psychology*, 62, 34–37.

Jackofsky, E.F. & Peters, L.H. (1987). Part-time vs full-time employment status differences: A replication and extension. *Journal of Occupational Behavior*, 8, 1–9.

Johnson, T. (1994). Telework: The challenge to organized labour's agenda. *Perception*, 18, 4–6.

Karasek, R.A. (1979). Job demands, job decision latitude, and mental strain: Implications for job redesign. *Administrative Sciences Quarterly*, 24, 43–48.

Kim, J.S. & Campagna, A.F. (1981). Effects of flexitime on employee attendance and performance: A field experiment. *Academy of Management Journal*, 24, 729–741.

Kingston, P.W. (1990). Illusions and ignorance about the family-responsive workplace. *Journal of Family Issues*, 11(4), 438–454.

Labour Canada. (1990). *Work life and personal needs: The job-sharing option*. Ottawa, Ontario: Human Resources Development Canada (Minister of Supply and Services Canada Catalogue No. L38-47/ 1990).

Lawton, M. & Brody, E. (1969). Assessment of older people. Self-maintaining and instrumental activities of daily living. *The Gerontologist*, 9, 179–186.

Lee, C., Duxbury, L., Higgins, C. & Mills, S. (1992). Strategies used by employed parents to balance the demands of work and family. *Optimum: The Journal of Public Sector Management*, 23, 67.

Leighton, P. (1991). The legal vulnerability of part-time workers: Is job sharing the solution? In M.J. Davidson & W. Earnshaw (Eds.), *Vulnerable workers: Psychological and legal issues* (pp. 279–296). Chichester:

John Wiley and Sons.

Lero, D.S. & Johnson, K.L. (1994). *110 Canadian statistics on work and family*. Ottawa, Ontario: The Canadian Advisory Council on the Status of Women.

Lero, D., Pence, A., Goelman, H. & Brockman, L. (1992). *Canadian national child care study*. Guelph, Ontario: University of Guelph, Department of Family Studies.

Martin Matthews, A., & Rosenthal, C.R. (1993). Balancing work and family in an aging society: The Canadian experience. In G.L. Maddox and M.P. Lawton (Eds.), *Annual Review of Gerontology and Geriatrics* pp. 96–119). New York: Springer.

McCubbin, H.I., Dahl, B. & Hunter, E.J. (1975). *Research on the military family: An assessment* (NTIS ADAO16 057). San Diego, CA: Naval Health Research Center.

McGuire, J.B. & Liro, J.R. (1987). Absenteeism and flexible work schedules. *Public Personnel Management*, **16**, 47–59.

Merderer, H.J. (1993). Division of labor in two-earner homes: Task accomplishment versus household management as critical variables in perceptions of family work. *Journal of Marriage and the Family*, **55**, 133–145.

Mott, P.E., Mann, F.C., Mclaughlin, Q. & Warwick, D.P. (1965). *Shiftwork: The social, psychological, and physical consequences*. Ann Arbor, MI: University of Michigan Press.

Narayanan, V.K. & Nath, R. (1982). A field test of some attitudinal and behavioral consequences of flextime. *Journal of Applied Psychology*, **67**, 214–218.

Neuman, G.A., Edwards, J.E. & Raju, N. (1989). Organizational development interventions: A meta-analysis of their effects on satisfaction and other attitudes. *Personnel Psychology*, **42**, 461–489.

Noble, B.P. (1994, July 31). Making family leave a reality. *The New York Times*, p. F19.

Nollen, S.D., Eddy, B.B. Hinder Marian, M.V. (1978). *Permanent part-time employment: The manager's perspective*. New York: Praeger.

Olmsted, B. & Smith, S. (1994). *Creating a flexible workplace*. New York: American Management Association.

Orpen, C. (1981). Effect of flexible working hours on employee satisfaction and performance: A field experiment. *Journal of Applied Psychology*, **66**, 113–115.

Partridge, B. E. (1973). Notes on the impact of flextime in a large insurance company II: Reactions of supervisors and managers. *Occupational Psychology*, **47**, 241–242.

Ronen, S. (1981). Arrival and departure patterns of public sector employees before and after implementation of flexitime. *Personnel Psy-*

chology, **34**, 817–822.

Ronen, S. & Primps, S.B. (1980). The impact of flextime on performance and attitudes in 25 public agencies. *Public Personnel Management*, **9**, 201–207.

Smulders, P.G.W. (1993). Absenteeism of part-time and full-time employees. *Applied Psychology: An International Review*, **43**, 239–252.

Solomon, C.M. (1994). Work/family's failing grade: Why today's initiatives aren't enough. *Personnel Journal*, **73**(4), 72–87.

Statistics Canada. (1991). *Report on the demographic situation in Canada*. Ottawa, Canada: Catalogue No. 91–209E Minister of Supply and Services.

Thomas, L.T. & Ganster, D.C. (1995). Impact of family-supportive work variables on work-family conflict and strain: A control perspective. *Journal of Applied Psychology*, **80**, 6–15.

Thompson L. & Walker, A.J. (1989). Gender in families: Women and men in marriage, work and parenthood. *Journal of Marriage and the Family*, **51**, 845–71.

Watson Wyatt Memorandum. (1995). *1995 work and family survey: Key themes*. Toronto, Ontario: Watson Wyatt Worldwide

Work Family Directions (1993). *Workplace flexibility: A strategy for doing business*. Boston, MA: Work Family Directions.

Wotruba, T.R. (1990). Full-time vs. part-time salespeople: A comparison of job satisfaction, performance and turnover in direct selling. *International Journal of Research in Marketing*, **7**, 97–108.

Index

Index compiled by Annette Musker

9 780471 962281